To Bruno Nettl,

With sincere thanks for your help & support
over the years

Rob Simms

January 2004

The Repertoire of Iraqi Maqam

Rob Simms

The Scarecrow Press, Inc.
Lanham, Maryland, and Oxford
2004

SCARECROW PRESS, INC.

Published in the United States of America
by Scarecrow Press, Inc.
A wholly owned subsidiary of The Rowman & Littlefield Publishing Group, Inc.
4501 Forbes Boulevard, Suite 200, Lanham, Maryland 20706
www.scarecrowpress.com

PO Box 317
Oxford
OX2 9RU, UK

British Library Cataloguing in Publication Information Available

Library of Congress Cataloging-in-Publication Data

Simms, Rob, 1962–
  The repertoire of Iraqi maqam / Rob Simms.
    p. cm.
  Includes bibliographical references (p.   ), discography (p.   ), and index.
  ISBN 0-8108-4758-2 (alk. paper)
  1. Maqåam—Iraq. 2. Music—Iraq—History and criticism. I. Title.
ML3758.I7 S56 2004
780'.9567—dc21

                                                                2003013957

♾™ The paper used in this publication meets the minimum requirements of
American National Standard for Information Sciences—Permanence of
Paper for Printed Library Materials, ANSI/NISO Z39.48-1992.
Manufactured in the United States of America.

Dedicated to the spirit and freedom of the Iraqi people

Aman, aman

Contents

Alphabetical Listing of Maqam Anthology   vii

Introduction   1

Maqam in General and Iraqi Maqam in Particular   10

An Anthology of Iraqi Maqam   46

1   The Rast Family   47
     Rast   47
     Panjgah   59
     Sharqi Rast/Esfahan   62

2   The Beyat Family   64
     Beyat   64
     Bheirzawi   73
     Ibrahimi   76
     Juburi   79
     Mahmudi   81
     Mischin   83
     Mugabl   85
     Nari   87
     Sharqi Dogah   89
     Themes of Other Beyat Maqams   91

3   The Husseini Family   92
     Husseini   92
     Arwah   96
     Dasht   99
     Orfa   102

4   The Hijaz Family   104
     Hijaz Diwan   104
     'Araibun   111
     Hijaz Kar   114
     Homayun   117
     Huizawi   120
     Madmi   122
     Qatar   124
     Other Hijaz Maqams   126

5   The Saba Family   129
        Saba   129
        Hadidi   132
        Mansuri   134

6   The Segah Family   138
        Segah   138
        Awj   147
        Awshar   150
        Hakimi   153

7   The Nawa Family   156
        Nawa   156
        Khanabat   161
        Nahawand   163

8   The Ajam/Jahargah Family   165
        Ajam   165
        Jahargah   169
        Rashdi   172
        Taher   174

9   Miscellaneous Maqams   176
        Hleilawi   176
        Kurd   178
        Mukhalef   180

Glossary   187
Bibliography   188
Discography   191
General Index   192
Index of Modes   194
About the Author   197

Alphabetical Listing of Maqam Anthology

Ajam	165	Madmi	122
'Araibun	111	Mahmudi	81
Arwah	96	Mansuri	134
Awj	147	Mischin	83
Awshar	150	Mugabl	85
Beyat	64	Mukhalef	180
Bheirzawi	73	Nahawand	163
Dasht	99	Nari	87
Hadidi	132	Nawa	156
Hakimi	153	Orfa	102
Hijaz Diwan	104	Other Beyat Maqams	91
Hijaz Kar	114	Other Hijaz Maqams	126
Hleilawi	176	Panjgah	59
Homayun	117	Qatar	124
Huizawi	120	Rashdi	172
Husseini	92	Rast	47
Ibrahimi	76	Saba	129
Jahargah	169	Segah	138
Juburi	79	Sharqi Dogah	89
Khanabat	161	Sharqi Rast/Esfahan	62
Kurd	178	Taher	174

Introduction

It is my belief that city-Arab music generally is far behind Arab peasant music with regard to animation and originality. . . . The urban music frequently sounds stilted, affected, and artificial. . . . [But] the music of the Iraqi people [allegedly city musicians] did not at all lag behind the most interesting peasant music in terms of animation and vividness. Indeed the virtuosity and dramatic expression of these Iraqi musicians made their performances one of the highlights of the concerts.

—Bela Bartok[1]

The tradition of Iraqi maqam has received relatively scant attention in the large body of Western literature concerning "maqam cultures." While the murderous strife of the past decades accounts for its recent neglect, one wonders why Iraqi maqam was left out of the wave of research on West Asian modal traditions that characterized Western, particularly American, ethnomusicology in the 1960s and 1970s. The wealth of scholarly attention devoted to Persian music at that time likely reflects the cozy relations enjoyed between the United States and the Shah, whereas Iraq kept closer ties with the Soviet Union. American relations with Iraq spontaneously reversed after the 1979 Islamic Revolution in Iran, but by that time Western research of the tradition was inhibited by the Iran-Iraq War—a brutal eight-year stalemate in the trenches, strategically prolonged by illegal Western arms sales, that killed over one million people. Whatever the reasons may be, the resulting lack of public information regarding Iraqi maqam outside of Iraq is entirely out of step with the significance and value of the tradition, a unique gem of human expression. A fundamental problem in the existing literature is the absense of an adequately detailed, clear, and accessible exposition of the musical contents of the Iraqi maqam repertoire. The present study aims to begin filling this scholarly gap while providing listeners and musicians with a reference tool or rough road map for following, understanding, and appreciating both individual performances and the repertoire as a whole. Despite the title of the book and the fact that it presents a large number of maqams, this study does not include "the complete" repertoire, as this is impossible to establish; I describe, however, what may be considered the most important core of the tradition. My simple aim is to provide interested readers with a useful musicological reference source of the kind available for decades to students of Persian, Turkish, Arab, and Indian modal repertoires. Indeed, Bor's authoritative and user-friendly guide to North Indian *ragas* (1999) marks an auspicious beginning for a new generation of such reference tools. In spite of its present lack of professional glamour among scholars, there is still much basic, pedestrian work of this sort left undone that could help to remove basic ignorances in our understanding of the world's music.

Due to the wide distribution and popularity of their recordings, the tradition of classical Iraqi music best known outside its own borders is the solo 'oud school of Munir and Jamil Bashir, a relatively new style of music influenced by the virtuoso Sherif Muhiddin Haidar (1888–1967). Warkov (1987) has examined the instrumental taqsims of Iraqi immigrant musicians in Israel, a significant location of the Iraqi maqam tradition from 1950 to the mid-1980s, which are instrumental renditions modelled on the vocal repertoire. The genre seems relatively rare in both Iraq and Israel (see also Kojaman 2001, 124). Warkov's sample features condensed renditions that maintain the modulation scheme of the maqam but present no direct melodic correlation to the vocal model aside from the modally definitive opening section and some cadences. While I will not be examining this genre, the materials presented here provide a rich resource for such creative instrumental applications.

1

Maqam in Iraq primarily refers to a repertoire of ordered musical pieces, and only secondarily to melodic modes in general, thus reflecting Central Asian usage of the term. In some ways I perpetuate a common confusion regarding Iraqi maqam by focusing here upon the role of melodic modes and form in the repertoire rather than the other complex determinants of text (poetry, vocables, and interjections) and rhythmic accompaniment that also define individual maqams. Traditional performers of Iraqi maqam have used a highly localized, unique, and practical vocabulary to describe and transmit their music, and few were cognizant of modal abstraction, which was grafted onto the tradition in the 1950s by theorists familiar with Mashreqi modal theory (Scheherazade Hassan 2001, 547). While my primary objective is to describe the emic classification, I also follow this latter trend of approaching Iraqi music with the theoretical background of related classical traditions[2] for purposes of comparison and analysis. This is a delicate task, given Western scholarly proclivities for imposing classical or standardized modal theory on traditions where no such connections exist (Zeranska-Kominek 1992, 249–50). My view is that Mashreqi modal theory is a useful tool for analyzing and understanding features of the Iraqi tradition if used in moderation; there are instances when it is clearly inappropriate and irrelevant.

Iraqi maqam is a remarkably cosmopolitan musical tradition (Scheherazade Hassan 1989). With regard to form, performance practice, and modal repertoire, Iraqi maqam is related to, but distinct from, other Arab traditions and shows particularly strong links to Iran. Chabrier (1987, 161n7) noted how this related musical language crosses the ethno-cultural lines of Arab, Persian, and Turk (specifically Azeri, although there are clear influences of Ottoman music in Iraqi maqam as well). Very generally, Persian affinities center on form, hierarchical organization of repertoire, performance practice, and some melodic materials (themes, ornaments, cognate, and imported modes). Turkish/Mashreqi relationships concern modal materials and some features of transposition and modulation. Comparative remarks throughout this study are primarily intended as convenient points of reference, utilizing features of more familiar maqam cultures to help define and qualify Iraqi practices; I do not pursue the myriad historical complexities implied by such comparisons.

The discussion and descriptions in this study are limited to the secular Baghdadi school of maqam as it was represented from the 1920s to the mid-1970s, excluding religious styles and the lesser known repertoires of Kirkuk and Mosul. With a few exceptions, I also exclude detailed treatment of instrumental preludes and interludes, both composed and improvised, and strophic songs. Perhaps the most significant omission with regards to representing this music is that I do not deal with matters concerning poetry, which is central to the tradition, in any depth. I focus upon the artists and style of this period simply because I find the performances to be exceptionally beautiful, inspired, and reflective of a highly sophisticated level of musicianship. Despite the fact that the maqam tradition was being eclipsed by Egyptian-based mainstream styles at this time, scholars and amateur enthusiasts alike consider the recordings of this period to be canonical. Given the severe and brutal changes that have afflicted Iraqi culture in the last two decades, this study is in fact one of music history. The unique cultural milieu that fostered music in this period is gone, as are the great musicians of the era. Considering the relentless horrors suffered by the Iraqi people (which seem destined only to intensify as I write these lines [September 2002]) and their struggle simply to survive, it is morally difficult to contemplate issues such as what may remain today of the maqam tradition. Many musicians and enthusiasts are pessimistic about the future. International recording artist Hamid al-Saadi, a student of the eminent reciter[3] Yusuf Omar, feels that the tradition has ended due to the lack of an informed audience and reliable patronage (Kojaman 2001, 50). This bleak conclusion is open to debate, however: Scheherazade Hassan reports of excellent performers, young and old, who are "only known within traditional circles both secular and religious" (2001, 555; personal communication, 2002). The destiny of this remarkable music is surely in their hands. The present study was in no wise conceived as an exercise in 'salvage musicology' but rather one of applied theory, music appreciation, and music history. Originally designed for my own use as a means of exploring my private collection of maqam recordings, I felt that it could be useful to others and help promote an increased awareness of this inspiring facet of Iraqi culture. This music offers us a sorely needed, sympathetic insight into the collective soul of the Iraqi people.

Christopher Small was right, of course: "music is not a thing at all but an activity" (1998, 2). Still, many of us are interested in the structural and practical means by which performers musick in the Iraqi tradition. My musicking is that of the maqam enthusiast (*ushshaq al-maqam*) spending much of my time listening to this music and discussing it within a circle of enthusiasts (*halaqat al-maqam*) [Scheherazade Hassan 1996, 4]. I was instantly attracted to recordings of Iraqi maqam and grew fascinated with its relationship to neighboring traditions, particularly Iranian. Listening, very careful listening, is generally the first step toward acquiring a working knowledge and performance ability of any music.

As music can be "taken and not necessarily given" in the traditional transmission of Iraqi maqam (Scheherazade Hassan 1996, 5; 2002, 313–14), my stalking, voyeuristic methods and closeted desires to be able to follow and perhaps perform this music are surprisingly emic. In this tradition it even seems culturally appropriate to appropriate an artist's intellectual property (cf., Bradley 1989). This is a local manifestation of the larger tradition of clandestine acquisition that extends at least through Iran, Central Asia, and North India, where it is often known as *poshte parde* (listening from "behind the curtain"). Knowledgeable musicians and enthusiasts make a clear distinction, however, between material that is learned directly from a master and that which was "sneaked" without the reciter's authorization (Scheherazade Hassan 1996, 5). The big difference is that a teacher can correct errors in the former scenario, while these go unchecked in the latter. All of the material in this book is the result of extensive sneaking. As the artists featured in this study are no longer alive, an ideal, collaborative study of their music is not possible (cf., Nelson 1991; Sorrell & Narayan 1980; Widdess 1994). While my sources and methodology are admittedly limited and errors are inevitable under such conditions, this study nonetheless reveals a great deal about the musical structure of Iraqi maqam.

The use of recordings as a means of musical transmission and acquisition is a global phenomenon, a perfectly natural facilitator of feedback within the complex system of a musical culture (and between cultures). Recording technology in general can be viewed as self-similar feedback wherein we share, reuse, and recontextualize a past moment at which we are paradoxically both present and absent. In the tradition of Iraqi maqam, no less a figure than Yusuf Omar made diligent study of the recordings of Mohammed Qubanchi early in his training; in this case, the admiration became mutual.[4] Omar openly acknowledged the importance and efficacy of recordings in the process of transmission (Kojaman 2001, 74).

Research and Sources

In the West, preliminary ethnomusicological spadework describing the broadest outlines of Iraqi maqam began with Tsuge's short article (1972), which provided a list of maqams, outlined basic structural features, and emphasized relationships to Persian classical music (although some of these comparative comments are incorrect). Fleshing out basic structural, social, and historical features of the tradition has been continued, almost single-handedly, by Scheherazade Hassan in a series of articles and valuable recording notes beginning in the 1980s. Wegner's detailed work on South Iraqi folk recitation (1982) deserves mention, as there are some structural similarities between this tradition and the urban art of maqam, and even occasional borrowings from the former into the latter.[5] Esther Warkov's dissertation (1987) centers on the complex historical and social aspects of the Iraqi immigrant community in Israel and is not devoted exclusively to the Iraqi maqam but nonetheless contains much important information on the same. Ogger (1987) includes a detailed analysis of Yusuf Omar's performance of maqam Segah (from OCR 79), which is of an etic nature that omits discussion of the important emic concept of qit'a (component melody or submode of a maqam). Elsner (1992) translates from Arabic into German some useful passages regarding the general structure of Iraqi maqam from Hashim Rijab's seminal study and provides a comparative study of maqam Rast (1983). Touma (1996) briefly recapitulates basic features of the tradition and includes a useful analysis of Yusuf Omar's recording of maqam Mansuri (from Philips 6586006). Aside from Tsuge's cursory outline, Elsner's translations regarding modal theory, and Scheherazade Hassan's liner notes to Yusuf Omar's recordings, these studies tend to focus on the contents of a single maqam in isolation. This is an interesting scholarly parallel to the fact that, due to the intricacies and complexities of Iraqi maqam, most performers know only a few maqams and very few learn the entire repertoire. Kojaman (2001) is the most recent contribution to the literature, based on his unfinished dissertation at the University of London and privately published with two CDs.[6] This study provides a detailed ethnography of maqam performance contexts, historical information regarding the first half of the twentieth century (including an interesting collection of photos), some musical analyses, and the valuable commentary of contemporary musicians Hamid al-Saadi and Bahir Rijab. Kojaman presents the most comprehensive listing to date of the repertoire and its components but is limited in describing musical structure, as his perspective is primarily that of a connoisseur and social historian, not a musician (2001, 7–9).

Fortunately this relatively small body of Western scholarship is balanced by a wealth of sources published in Iraq, which are reviewed by Scheherazade Hassan (1992a); collectively they provide a fine foundation for acquiring an understanding of the music. Written in Arabic, the intended audience of this literature is decidedly local[7] and knowledge of it has been largely restricted to a small group of specialist scholars in the West. Cultural outsiders interested in exploring this "Other musicology" (Qureshi 2001) must take several factors into consideration. Levels of the authors' familiarity with the technical aspects of the maqam tradition may vary widely, ranging from amateur enthusiasts and journalists with limited musical abilities to professional scholars of various disciplines and renowned performers of the maqam tradition. Modes of presentation and explication often differ from those of Western scholarly sensibilities and conventions, and local contextual, insider information may be assumed tacitly by the authors. Historical, biographical, and textual aspects of the tradition often receive more emphasis than theoretical or structural features of music. In terms of the focus of the present study, the most relevant and useful written Iraqi sources are the following: Ibrahim Sha'oubi al-Khalil's[8] *Dalil al-angham li tullab al-maqam* ("Guide of Melodies for Students of Maqam") (1982); Hashim Rijab's *Al-maqam al-'Iraqi* (1983 edition); and Bahir Rijab's (Hashim's son) *Usul ghina' al maqam al-Baghdadi* ("Basis of Singing the Baghdadi Maqam") (1985).

According to Kojaman (2001, 48–49), instrumental accompaniment of Iraqi maqam during the first half of the twentieth century was monopolized by two ensembles, each under the leadership of a Jewish musical family: the Pataos and Bassuns. Sha'oubi and Hashim Rijab were among the first non-Jewish musicians to learn instrumental practice after the mass exodus of Iraqi Jews to Israel in 1950, which resulted in a greater number of instrumentalists within the Baghdadi maqam tradition. Sha'oubi (1925–1991) was an eminent performer of the joze (spike fiddle) who eventually taught maqam repertoire at the Institute of Melodic Studies (a branch of the Ministry of Culture) in Baghdad throughout the 1970s and 1980s. His book is based on his teaching materials, centering on recorded performances of forty maqams in simplified versions, published with six one-hour cassettes (featuring the author as vocalist, accompanying himself on joze, along with an anonymous percussionist). The text supplies general information about the repertoire and verbal descriptions for each maqam performance along with some transcriptions. The study ingeniously emphasizes the aural experience, as the locations of musical structures are indexed to the text of the poem; one must listen and not merely read the text passively. Sha'oubi is the most comprehensive survey of the contents of the Baghdadi repertoire and for many minor maqams the only detailed source that clearly identifies maqam components; for this reason the present study draws heavily upon this valuable source. As the two performed together for years, Sha'oubi generally corroborates Yusuf Omar's performances. Understandable, but nonetheless frustrating, is the fact that Sha'oubi was an instrumentalist and not a singer; his renditions are pedagogical and cannot be compared to the artistic performances of the great reciters of the period. A significant problem throughout Sha'oubi's work is the frequent discrepencies between pitches prescribed or described in his text and the actual intonation of his performance on the recordings. The recordings also suffer from a relatively poor recording quality and choppy editing, particularly frequent mid-performance "punch-in" edits. Scheherazade Hassan has questioned the value of Sha'oubi's presentation, rightly noting its effect of propogating simplified, standardized versions of what was traditionally a varied, complex, and evolving repertoire (1992, 264–65). "Due to the diversity of schools and trends, there is no one definite version of any maqam nor is there a consensus about which version one should start with. The idea of a simplified version free of ornaments and difficult segments is unknown in traditional learning and has only appeared with formal modern classes" (1996, 10).

When the Iraqi government assumed the official patronage and control of maqam transmission in the 1970s they arbitrarily favored musicians literate in Western notation, which effectively excluded and alienated the reciters, who were the true guardians of the tradition. Furthermore, the government-sponsored Iraqi Musical Heritage Ensemble toured extensively performing and propagating simplified versions of maqams that were designed to be accessible to audiences ignorant of the intricacies of the maqam tradition (Scheherazade Hassan, 1995). Nationalistic interests are evident in the tendency to alter passages traditionally sung in foreign languages (Turkish, Persian, Kurdish, Hebrew), which were either omitted or changed to Arabic; apparently Sha'oubi was compelled by authorities to alter the renditions of his text against his will (Kojaman 2001, 69, 162–63). While these developments are indeed problematic (and unfortunate, to many maqam enthusiasts), I also see the bird's-eye-view advantage of such simplified, concise versions, at least when one is trying to get an initial grasp of such a rich and complex tradition. Like the novice backyard astronomer, it is better to begin stargazing guided by simplified star maps, as detailed ones are usually overwhelming.

H. Rijab (1983) is the most widely cited reference in the scholarship of Iraqi maqam, describing history, theory, performance practice, and repertoire. B. Rijab (1985) contains general information as well as useful transcriptions of 30 qit'as and seven basic maqams; the transcriptions were apparently formulated through deducing essential structures from various authoritative performers, including those of his father. Another useful source for this study is Thamir al-Amiri's *Al-maqam al-'Iraqi* (1990), which includes texual descriptions of a large portion of the repertoire, historical and cultural contexts of individual maqams, and transcriptions (made by Ruhi al-Khammash) of thirteen different maqams recorded by famous reciters. Unfortunately, the recordings for these transcriptions are difficult to obtain.

The recorded performances of three great twentieth-century reciters—Rashid Qundarchi (1885–1945), Mohammed Qubanchi (1901–1989), and Yusuf Omar (1918–1987)—selections of which have been released relatively recently on wide-distribution French labels, form another important source for this study. Apart from his idiosyncratic falsetto, Qundarchi's style was conservative and he was antagonistic toward Qubanchi's free and innovative approach to the repertoire; despite modelling himself on Qubanchi, Yusuf Omar was also conservative (Scheherazade Hassan 1992, 124–25, 1995a, 17; Moussali 1996, 40–41). With exceptions due to individual interpretation and affiliation to stylistic schools, the sources are remarkably consistent, often down to melodic details. In a few cases where the sources differ significantly, I have consulted difficult-to-obtain bootleg recordings of the same reciters.

Selecting these recorded sources leads to questions regarding the role of women in the twentieth-century tradition of Iraqi maqam performance. As with many classical West Asian traditions, women were disadvantaged because the primary venues for public maqam performance and transmission in the first half of the twentieth century were exclusively male preserves. In the secular tradition these included the coffeehouse and, according to van der Linden (1999, 4), the *zurkhane* (gymnasium). On the other hand, the most important venue was, and still is, gatherings in private homes, where women are present.[9] There are also suggestions within the tradition of a masculine quality intrinsic to the music and singing style itself, restricting successful performance to men (e.g., Hamid al-Saadi quoted in Kojaman [2001, 127]).[10] While female vocalists were active throughout the twentieth century in Iraq, particularly after 1930, their participation in the maqam repertoire was extremely limited and generally centered on the popular, modern repertoire associated with nightclubs. In terms of public female figures, Sadiqqa al-Mullayya (1901–1968), Zuhur Hussein, and Ma'ida Nazhat (b. 1937) each recited a few maqams from the traditional repertoire; Farida Mohammed Ali (b. 1963) is the first woman to devote herself to the repertoire (Scheherazade Hassan, personal communication, 2002). Uncredited liner notes to Farida's CD *Muwal and Maqamat Iraqi* (Sam CD 9001) maintain that a tradition of female recitation exists in Kerbala and elsewhere in the Shi'a south.

This study consolidates, cross-references, re-presents, and reorganizes Iraqi sources in order to present more conveniently the information latent in these materials, and to provide a useful reference for identifying and studying performances of Iraqi maqam. While they certainly do not tell the whole story, Sha'oubi and the Rijabs are valuable, pedagogically advantageous starting points. Qundarchi, Qubanchi, and Omar are unquestionably the most important reciters of their time. What hopefully emerges in the present work is an overall view of the basic musical features of a great art music tradition, little known outside Iraq, as represented by a few key individuals of the twentieth century.

Transcription and Transliteration

While B. Rijab (1985) and al-Amiri (1991) feature extensive transcriptions, Iraqi sources more frequently describe melodies and formal schemes verbally[11] rather than by means of musical notation. Sha'oubi (1982) contains some notated examples (particularly scales and pasta repertoire) but largely bypasses notation by indexing materials to corresponding lines of poetry in his demonstration cassettes. Given the intricacies and subtleties of the vocal art of Iraqi maqam, it is easy to understand why traditional oral/aural methods have been retained to transmit this music: it is indeed the most efficacious (and likely the only accurate) means of doing so. Due to subjective perceptions, limitations of notation, and the inherent richness and depth of the music, my transcription of the same music often changes from one listening to the next. As Keith Jarrett put it, in a very rare instance of a performer editing the published transcription of his own improvisation, all too often we must "choose between alternate inaccuracies" (Jarrett 1991, preface). This begs the question: Why transcribe music that inevitably eludes the quantitative confines of notation? For those who can read notation I believe that it makes certain structural features more readily apparent and discernable, allows for certain comparative and analytical observations outside the flow of time, facilitates the memory of musical materials, and can help one locate and follow the series of events that occur in a long performance. Some benefits only go to the transcriber—a kind of brainwashing that etches the musical language and details deeply into the mind, resulting in a certain degree of competence along with some generative sensibilities. Transcription increases the speed and volume of musical transmission compared to traditional oral means, differing radically in both quality (i.e., it is less accurate) and quantity (places a larger repertoire at one's fingertips). It is yet another accelerated means of system feedback within a musical culture, an admittedly limited tool or road map that has the potential to deepen our understanding of various levels of musical structure. If taken too seriously, however, transcription can stifle individual creativity and stylistic diversity, and if treated too casually it can lead to fleeting, superficial perceptions of deep and complex traditions.

It is difficult, if not impossible, to establish an abstract theory of maqam because our understanding of it is necessarily mediated by the performances and conceptions of individual musicians. In the Iraqi tradition individual artists not only have their own styles and arrangements of the repertoire, but the same artist may realize a particular maqam in varied ways from one performance to the next. Other than the materials taken from B. Rijab (1985), all of the transcriptions in this study are of particular performances, an artist's individual and perhaps idiosyncratic interpretation of a maqam. To further confound the notion of a rigorously objective understanding of maqam, any transcription represents a set of essentially arbitrary choices, limitations, and emphases imposed by the transcriber. My transcriptions privilege the vocal soloist at the expense of the instrumental parts. I have formatted the transcriptions to reveal melodic, modal, and formal structure, features that can be delineated reasonably clearly using modified Western notation, in a format appropriated by some Iraqi musicians themselves. The graphic notation used by Touma (1976, 30) and Wegner (1982) is very effective for this style of music but I have decided to follow the conventional Iraqi format of notation, which is arguably more precise for representing complex melismata. The notation I use is inadequate for representing features that are essential to this music, particularly rhythm, ornamentation, and timbre. While I have made a small number of arbitrations, the transcriptions are not able to convey the difference between what was intended and what was executed by the performer. The amount of time and care devoted to each transcription was uneven; completed over a period of five years, some are the result of six or seven carefully revised drafts (e.g., Hijaz Diwan, Yusuf Omar's Rast), others received three less intense revisions (e.g., Nawa, Kurd).[12] Useful software programs (such as Transcribe) only came to my attention when finishing the project and were not used in the transcription process. I am presenting a repertoire mediated by a specific commercial recording, an individual artist, the unique rendition of the performer at the recording session, and my transcription technique. It goes without saying that we are left with a dim and incomplete shadow of the music itself. When used with the sound recordings, however, these transcriptions will enhance one's appreciation and understanding of certain melodic, modal, and formal parameters. With the unfortunate exception of Sha'oubi (which really needs to be digitally restored and reissued), these recordings are readily available.

Two types of transcription are used in this study: full and reductive. The latter are designed in the spirit of Schenkerian analyses minus the rigid methodology; as with Schenker's original intentions, my reductions are not presented as abstract theory but are designed to inform performance and music appreciation. They aim at abstracting features that reveal the melodic and formal framework underlying the performance. Indeed, in some instances "writing down all the notes would give more of a false view . . . than selecting some notes" (Jarrett 1991, preface). Noteheads in the reductive transcriptions indicate very general relative duration, a format that conveniently reveals pitch hierarchy and melodic contour. A shorthand notation is used occasionally that indicates the range of a melody filled in with a line. In such instances the intervening melody consists of essentially stepwise motion or it repeats material previously transcribed in greater detail. All transcriptions from Sha'oubi (1982) are based on his recordings and not the verbal descriptions of his text; while some vocables and interjections are indicated I have not included the poetic text in these transcriptions.

The nature of the free rhythm idiomatic of Iraqi singing is such that, even when accompanied by a set metric cycle, vocal articulations often fall between the cracks of regular pulse. The beauty of this style lies in this naturally flowing irregularity. Transcriptions of rhythmic maqams (see p. 35 below) make no attempt to coordinate the vocal line with the rhythmic cycle. Beaming and note groupings are designed to reflect rhythmic weight and stress. Durational values are qualitative and not quantitative: a quarter note is "longer" than an eighth note but "shorter" than a dotted quarter note, and so on. Assigning a unit from among these broad gradations is of course subjective and open to interpretation.

Symbols standardized in Arab music publication are used for *kar* ("quarter-tone") flats and sharps; in the text *kar bimol* half-flats are represented with the sign ♭. Additional symbols include: ʌ v for neighbor note embellishments and mordents (upper and lower); ∿∿∿ for wide vibrato or continuously repeated neighbor; and ∽ indicating turns or ornamentation that occurs both above and below main pitch. Symbols are placed to indicate roughly when the ornaments occur—on or after the initial attack—and are only indicated once per note, even if two or more ornaments occur in the performance; there is no indication of the rhythmical features of ornaments, which may vary considerably in performance. These marks are ornamental and can be ignored without detracting from the main purpose of the transcriptions, that is, outlining the melodic contour, modal definition, and form of a maqam. Neighbor note and turn figures are transcribed unabbreviated when they constitute an integral, nondecorative motive. Phrases are separated by a short tick at the top of the staff. Vocal sections (defined here as units separated by instrumental interludes [*muhasiba*], which are not transcribed unless they include important thematic or cadential material) are numbered and end with a barline (again, aside from clearly marked exceptions, barlines in rhythmic maqams do not demarcate the rhythmic cycle). The full transcriptions, which attempt to show the musical foreground in order to guide listening and promote an appreciation of the individual stylistic elements of master performers, employ the same phrase and sectional markings along with the standard Western signs designating articulation.

Glottal ornaments are indicated with a small circle (*o*), the conventional Persian sign for the *tekye*; a lighter glottal ornament or short pulsation is indicated with a staccato dot. The standard symbol for the trill denotes (but does not differentiate between) rapid, continuous neighbor-note motion or extended glottal pulsation. Scale degrees are given as ciphers without the conventional superscript caret (^). Underlined ciphers (6) denote pitches below the tonic, apostrophes (3'), pitches an octave above the tonic. Scoops and slurred articulation are indicated by conventional markings; extended portamento and glissandi are denoted by straight lines. These should not be confused with the use in reductive transcriptions, where, as mentioned above, straight lines connecting disjunct pitches indicate that the melody proceeds stepwise through all intermediate pitches of the outlined interval.

The maqam anthology is ordered according to the basic maqams beginning with maqam Rast and proceeding by tonic pitch families, followed by their respectively derived offspring. While my exposition focuses on melodic materials and form, the reader should bear in mind the other determinants of text and rhythmic accompaniment not emphasized here. In some examples only new materials are exposed. The reappearance of material in new contexts (i.e., different maqams) are not reproduced if they are performed with substantial consistency: they are merely noted and qualified by indicating transposition from conventional pitch levels, and illustrated by outlining the essential contour in the transcription. This is particularly applicable to Sha'oubi's performances presented here. While there are many common features for grouping related maqams in the repertoire, each is unique (like individual people) and must be approached on individual terms, paying close attention to exceptions and idiosyncracies. Hamid al-Saadi's listings for words assigned to individual maqam components are from Kojaman (2001, 171–76, 200–207).

Schematic diagrams of each maqam are provided to summarize their contents and formal structure as rendered in the particular performance. Components are listed in the order they occur on the top line, under which their melodic focus is indicated by scale degree ciphers (based on the scale degrees of the maqam's main modality, regardless of modulation). A dotted line indicates that the components are juxtaposed in the same section of recitation of the performance. If a particular component involves a modulation that alters intervallic structures, the new tetrachord name or altered pitch is indicated below the line of ciphers: Beyat/3 is therefore a modulation to the tetrachord of Beyat beginning on the third degree of the original scale. The relative lengths of sections and successive repetitions of sections are not indicated; diagram units are merely sized to accommodate the text. The metric cycle of rhythmically accompanied maqams is given on the last line, placed to indicate where the accompaniment begins and ends throughout the course of the maqam.

Component 1	Comp. 2	Comp. 3	Comp. 4	Comp. 5	Comp. 6	Comp. 7
Melodic range (in ciphers)	4–1	8-1-5-1	6-8-5	3-1	3-6-2	5-1
	Scale change		Beyat/3			
Rhythmic accompaniment						

Transliterations are designed for readers of English to replicate approximately the pronunciation of the Iraqi dialect without the cumbersome use of diacritical markings and specialized symbols. Frequently used terms are treated as English loan words: they are not italicized and are rendered plural with the English marker "s." While some may view this negatively, my simple intention is to make the text (and, by extension, the tradition of Iraqi maqam itself) accessible and respectfully unexotic to a wide range of readers (cf., Guenon 1945, 184). To avoid further cluttering already congested transcriptions, I have omitted the conventional use of lines to denote extended syllables in textual underlay: pitches with no indication of text prolong the previous syllable. Poetic texts were transcribed from the recordings without recourse to written editions; there are occasional elisions in the transcriptions when the text is questionable or unintelligible.

Acknowledging Limitations and Invaluable Assistance

From an ideal, integral view of Iraqi maqam, I have done some rather intense work in the "exterior-individual quadrant" with some comparative remarks that touch on the "exterior-collective" (Wilber 2000); the resulting perspective has all the grace and depth of an autopsy or anatomy lesson. It is clearly only a partial view, which is unbalanced but fine, providing one does not insist on the supremacy of these quadrants (and I don't). While this study contains detailed and hopefully useful transcriptions, a book can only supply information, not music, which requires the crucial element of play, the essentially mysterious, shamanic animation of an individual performer—precisely, the interior dimension. Of course, the whole point of music is that it takes us to a profound and special place that is inaccessible through words and visual symbols. The structure of Iraqi maqam, like a good many other musical things of the world, reflects the Taoist concept of *li* ("principle; organic pattern"): the irregularities in the patterns of jade markings, water turbulence, the configurations of stellar constellations, and so on. To impose upon them rigid geometric order or derivation distorts their true nature and entirely misses the point; order prevails but it defies neat, rigorous packaging. In contemporary translation the structure of Iraqi maqam is analog as opposed to digital, more fractal than Euclidean, or as the philosopher Alan Watts liked to express it, "wiggly, not straight." The greatest potential folly is to confuse symbols and classifications with real and direct experience and it is similarly a profound delusion to believe that by classifying and labelling things, we understand them. I have tried to maintain a balance between explicating basics of the emic Iraqi classification of the repertoire while avoiding the futility of *li*-mapping. The ultimate experience with music, after all, is to be carried away by it, a gift that thankfully defies and transcends explication. My attempt here stops well short of a comprehensive treatment of the subject (as far as such a thing is even possible), which I prefer to leave to Iraqi musicians and scholars. Indeed, Hashim Rijab's qualifications from forty years ago referring to contemporaneous Arab scholarship apply equally to the present study in our era of information, globalization, and the siege of Iraq. "This is not a complete study of this subject, and could not even be termed as a real introduction to such a long and complicated art. But it is a bird's eye view, to get people to know about this kind of music, about which nothing has been written so far. We hope that the reader will find this humble attempt as useful as it was intended to be" (1961, 10). If this study gets more people listening seriously to Iraqi maqam and provokes corrections and improvement by others (cf., Kippen 2002), it will have served its purpose.

I wish to thank sincerely Zeina Azouqah, Negin Bahrami, Mike Cado, Johanna Devaney, Mike D'Sa, Jim Kippen, Harold Powers, and Urszula Starzec for their assistance and support. I also thank the Social Sciences and Humanities Research Council of Canada and York University. The designers of Finale and Word software helped make my work a truly unforgettable, once-in-a-lifetime experience. Very special thanks to Scheherazade Hassan for her expertise, generosity, and dedicated research in Iraqi maqam, and to Saad al-Tayyar for his invaluable assistance on many fronts; this book would not exist without them. *Shukran.* My greatest appreciation and respect goes to the musicians of the Iraqi maqam tradition, both past and present, who are the true authorities and guardians of this great music. I sincerely apologize to them in advance for errors contained herein. May they soon sing of relief, freedom, and peace in the timeless cycle of human folly, destruction, and renewal that Mesopotamians surely know better than anyone under the sun. Royalties from this book are donated to Iraqi community development agencies.

Notes

1. Upon hearing Mohammed Qubanchi perform at the Congress of Arab Music, Cairo, 1932 (Suchoff 1976, 38–39). While this quote is interesting in and of itself, I deliberately begin with Bartok given the contents and perspective of this study. Despite the current fashion of bashing Bartok's work as an ethnomusicologist, I value his emphasis on extensive, careful listening and the creative application of research materials.

2. Which is apparently gaining currency in Iraq; the following section "Maqam Basics" provides an outline of these basic structures and principles.

3. A vocalist in the Iraqi maqam tradition is known as *qari'* ("reciter"), a prestigous terminological alignment with the tradition of Qur'an recitation.

4. "In an interview with the late Mohammed Al-Gubbenchi in the leading Alef-Ba' magazine, Al-Ustath Al-Gubbenchi was asked, 'who sang maqam after Mohammed Al-Gubbenchi?' He replied, 'Yousif Omar.' 'Who else but Yousif Omar?' asked the interviewer. 'Yousif Omar,' replied Al-Gubbenchi. 'Yes, but who else other than Yousif Omar?' insisted the interviewer. 'Yousif

Omar!' replied Mohammed Al-Gubbenchi again, showing how highly Mohammed Al-Gubbenchi thought of the late Yousif Omar (*sic*)." "Featured Artist–Yousif Omar," *Iraqimusic*, http://www.iraqimusic. com/featured (4 Dec. 2000).

5. Wegner observes that Iraqi theorists impose the modal system of maqam upon the folk traditions but the singers themselves deny its relevance (1982, 58–59). Similar dynamics characterize the relationship between Turkish makam and *ayak*, the modes of Turkish folk repertoires (Markoff 1989).

6. The CD includes six versions of maqam Segah and four versions of the famous pasta *'Afaki 'Afaki*, each performed by different reciters, an example of the sacred maqam repertoire, and a demonstration of iqa'at (metric cycles).

7. The first published information of substantial content on Iraqi maqam in a European language, however, was probably the ten-page English preface to Hashim Rijab's 1961 edition of *Al-maqam al-'Iraqi* (in Arabic), which shows an early interest in communicating to a wider audience.

8. His name is most frequently encountered in the literature as Sha'oubi Ibrahim, a practice that I will follow in this study.

9. See Kojaman 2001, 77–97 for a detailed description of a traditional *chalghi* evening of the 1930s or 1940s.

10. Masculine references in interjections such as *yaba* ("Oh father"), *ya ammi* ("Oh uncle"), *khayi* ("my brother"), *oghlem* ("my son"), and so on are routine. Some critics might regard the hierarchical structure of the repertoire itself as patriarchal.

11. See Warkov (1987, 225–26) for a typical verbal description in English translation.

12. The full transcriptions benefited from suggestions and revisions of Saad al-Tayyar, for which I am most grateful.

Maqam in General and Iraqi Maqam in Particular

Maqam means many things to many people (e.g., Elsner 1989, Elsner and Jähnichen 1992), making it extremely difficult and misleading to speak of "maqam in general." This part of the study provides background material for understanding the basic modal theory shared by many West Asian classical traditions and the specific principles and subtleties of Iraqi maqam.

Maqam Basics

While historical connections exist for much of the material presented in this section, the perspective here is aimed at making the assimilation and memory of structures and processes as easy as possible for the reader unfamiliar with maqam traditions (see also Marcus 2002; Signell 2002; Powers 1980, 422–28; and Feldman 1996, 195–273). The reader must bear in mind throughout this section that, like any theoretical perspective, it does not account for the wide range of variation found in the real world of creative music making. There is much more complexity and subtlety involved than this intentionally reductionist presentation suggests. I illustrate the discussion using largely Mashreqi nomenclature (which is close to that of contemporary Iraq); the basic structures and concepts have a wider application to maqam cultures in general: if one accepts variations of intonation, they present a core repertoire of cognate structures.[1] This perspective necessarily bulldozes the subtleties that are intrinsic to the local identities of specific maqams (During 2002, 855–56) in favor of revealing the general features of cognate families throughout West Asia. In very broad outline, modern traditions show a continuity with ancient Near Eastern structures and ideas as they existed in the consolidated form inherited by the Greeks: microtonal intervals, the primacy of the tetrachord, the generative potential of octave species, and preset melodic formulae.

In his global survey Powers suggests that modes exist within a continuum between the extremes of an abstract scale and a specific tune (and by extension, an entirely prescribed composition) (1980, 377, 422). Indian *ragas* lie somewhere around the midpoint of this continuum, while maqam traditions sweep across its entirety. Very generally Iraqi, Iranian, and Central Asian classical traditions lean toward the tune pole, Mashreqi and Maghrebi maqams the scale pole, with Turkish hovering around the middle. Classical maqams are defined and transmitted through canonical repertoires that are generally analogous to the Western concept of a composition, or more precisely, a composed suite. Some of these canons may be performed as an end in themselves (e.g., Iraq, Central Asia, the Maghreb), others function in this manner but also are used as models from which one inductively acquires improvisatory materials and strategies (e.g., Turkey, the Mashreq). The Persian radif is a rather unique canon in that it is a mixture of music theory, repertoire, and practical pedagogy—an organized collection of melodic formulae that function as models for composition and improvisation. The radif is not performed as an end in itself but rather practiced as a means to the end of creating individualized, unique musical expressions. While most classical canons consist of metrical compositions, the radif and Iraqi maqam for the most part feature a free, recitative-like rhythm. The following outline focuses on structures and processes, but the most immediate and essential feature of maqam is the evocation of a specific Affekt or atmosphere; mode and mood are integrally and definitively related.

Intervals, Pitch Designation, Tetrachords, and Scales

As with the Greeks and in medieval Europe, much West Asian music theory was concerned with tuning theory, the historical evolution of which is exceedingly complex. Given leeway for microtonal variation, the intervals used in modern music can be conceived etically in three generic types: whole and half tones (diatonic); three-quarter tones; and augmented seconds. We may summarize this collection with the three tetrachords Ajam, Rast, and Hijaz (**ex. 1.1**).

In contrast to the prickly mathematical descriptions that generally occupy theorists, musicians are naturally more intuitive and spontaneous. Empirical studies such as Farhat (1991, 15–18) and During (1985) illustrate a fairly wide range of variation and tolerance in intonation among Persian musicians that seems typical of other West Asian traditions (the Turkish classical tradition is the most discriminating in this respect). Perhaps the most concise and practical guideline, sufficient for the purposes of this study, is to envision the so-called "neutral" second as dividing a minor third in half; likewise a "neutral" third lies at the approximate midpoint of a perfect fifth. Among other complications, intonation usually varies with modal context: the same pitch may be tuned differently as it functions in different modes. Again, such adjustments are made intuitively by musicians after years of training and immersion in the music.

Whether following ancient Greek theory or perhaps because early Arab music theorists designated pitch in relation to finger positions on the 'oud, individual pitches are traditionally assigned proper names. Most modern classical traditions are oriented toward middle C—the pitch named Rast ("rectitude")—as the main reference or fulcrum of the system. Turkish theory presents an important exception to this, sharing most of the same pitch names but equating Rast to G above middle C. The assignment of pitch names goes beyond the Western and Indian notions of solfege and *sargam* in that chromatic and microtonal pitches are not denoted as alterations of a diatonic scale degree, but rather as discrete entities. So, for example, the pitch F♮ in the Arab tradition is denoted Jahargah, while F♯ is Hijaz; E♭ is Kurd, while E♭ is Segah and E♮ is Buselik. And unlike solfege or *sargam*, pitch names do not always replicate at the octave, so that the upper octave of the pitch Rast (middle C) is Kardaniye, the B♭ below Rast is Iraq while its upper octave is Awj. Furthermore, these designations do not necessarily refer to absolute pitch but are often relative in the manner of *sargam* and movable-doh solfege. The result of this system is that certain tetrachords are assigned to specific pitches in both theory and practice, and while certain transpositions are possible, one must begin by learning the basic "root" position of the tetrachord. Throughout this study I will identify pitches as degrees of a particular scale using Arabic numeral ciphers or a corresponding Western designation (C, E♭, F♯, etc.). Indeed, while maqam traditions retain the traditional names of tetrachords, scales, and maqams with their corresponding root positions, the traditional pitch nomenclature has been largely supplanted by Western solfege syllables, which may function variously as fixed or movable-doh systems depending on the context. Chromatic and microtonal pitches are usually described as alterations of diatonic scale degrees (often both solfege and traditional nomenclature are given in theoretical discussions). Many names of tetrachords and maqams correspond to the traditional names of individual pitches, most frequently denoting the first note of the tetrachord (e.g., the root position of the tetrachord Rast begins on the pitch Rast). The bottom tetrachord of a maqam scale, at least with the most basic and important maqams, frequently denotes name of the maqam itself (e.g., Rast, Ajam, and Hijaz[2]).

Understanding maqam necessitates thinking in terms of tetrachords, from the most elementary stages of acquaintance to advanced levels of performance. The ambitus of most melodies and the construction of scales in West Asian music are frequently defined by tetrachords, which are also the basis for comprehending and commanding the language of modulation. Indeed, the concept of scale or maqam is often subordinate to that of tetrachord, notably in the repertoire of Mevlevi ritual music, which is difficult to perform without vigilantly monitoring this structural level. While various rosters and systems have been proposed by theorists (cultural insiders and outsiders alike), it is possible to derive virtually all tetrachords and maqam scales in current use from the tetrachords listed in ex. 1.1. Derivations are based on the octave species phasing, a characteristic of Arab music theory since before al-Farabi (d. 950 A.D.), whose system exploited this logical generative process (Sawa 1989, 85–91).[3] It is necessary to expand the elemental unit of the tetrachord to a heptatonic scale in order to generate complete tetrachords for each phase of the original (and paradoxical that tetrachords, the essence of maqam, are here derived from scales). The maqam scales, whose names correspond to those of the fundamental tetrachords are given in **ex. 1.2**. Rast has ascending and descending forms; like the Western melodic minor scale, the variable pitches are raised when ascending and lowered when descending.

The most important tetrachord species generated from the Ajam scale are Nahawand and Kurd (**ex. 1.3**). The fourth species is rather rare in West Asia and not found in this position—when transposed to the pitch Rast it implicitly appears in the Turkish and Mashreqi maqam Panjgah and the Maghrebi *tubu'* Rast al-dhil.[4] The scale of Rast further yields two important tetrachords. The usage of Segah in maqam repertoire is such that it frequently appears as a simple trichord E♭-G (**ex. 1.4**). Hijaz supplies the pentachord Nikris/Nagriz (**ex. 1.5**).

Since the modern period of Arab music theory beginning in the late-nineteenth century (see Marcus 1989), maqam scales have been described by the mixing and matching of the basic tetrachords outlined above; most tetrachords are disjunct and transposed to 5 for the upper components. **Ex. 1.6** shows the most fundamental maqam scales with their component tetrachords organized by "tonic families" (C tonic, D tonic, etc.); while the standard Arab nomenclature is used here, there are (with compromises regarding microtuning) cognates of most of these scale types throughout West Asia. Some scales include ascending and descending forms. The intervallic structure of basic maqam scales can be conveniently conceptualized and memorized through octave species phasing of the three scale families Rast, Hijaz, and Ajam (**ex. 1.7**). Some species use either ascending or descending forms of the original scale, which are indicated below by their placement on the ascent or descent of the original (e.g., Bayati as the second octave species of the descending form of Rast is indicated on the descending scale degree).

Modal Functions, Processes, and Form

Having outlined basic tonal materials in the preceding section we now turn to the theoretical transformation of scales into modes. As with Indian *ragas*, many maqams share the same scale but are differentiated by melodic considerations brought about by the particular qualities or functions of individual scale degrees. Many of the modal parameters discussed below were at least partially explicated by Demetrius Cantemir (writing around 1700) and gained wider currency among maqam theorists in the nineteenth and early twentieth century; others were posited by modern theorists. For comparative purposes I will discuss these functions in generic English with only occasional references to emic terminology. These functions are better viewed as likely and definitive tendencies rather than rigidly consistent prescriptions; various traditions place different emphasis on particular functions.

Maqams are identified by the contour of their background (and/or middle ground) *melodic progressions*. This is most explicitly theorized in the Turkish tradition (known as *seyir*), where makams are categorized as having ascending, descending, or ascending-descending progressions. *Ascending* progressions are essential arcs that begin on 1, eventually ascend through the upper octave and return to 1. *Descending* progressions begin in the upper octave and eventually descend to 1. *Ascending-descending* progressions begin in the midrange, ascend through the upper octave, and return to 1. Successive phrases and formal periods of the maqam repeat the progression, creating a more or less undulating effect at the middle ground level. What sounds neat and tidy in theoretical terms is in reality a much more complex, perhaps even chaotic, phenomenon. One must study and ideally memorize many compositions in the same maqam to grasp inductively the nature of a particular progression, particularly in Arab and Turkish traditions. Individual idiosyncracies, definitive subtleties, and creative possibilities aside, the three traditional Turkish *seyir* templates are indeed adequate for describing large-scale melodic progression. *Start, stop,* and *final note* functions are self-explanatory and another means of defining melodic progression—maqams are differentiated by which scale degrees serve as points of starting, stopping, or resting midway through, or finishing a phrase. These functions are not necessarily the tonic, as one might expect. In general, modes are essentially hierarchical and certain degrees receive more or less relative emphasis or weight. A particular pitch (other than the tonic) will receive the *greatest emphasis*; another pitch *secondary emphasis*; in vocal genres these often function as *recitation tones* for delivering text in the most expedient manner. Highest and lowest notes to which the maqam normally extends may be generically termed as *apogee* and *perigee. Ambitus* or *range* is a definitive feature of some maqams; while most extend over an octave, some feature a narrower melodic range. *Chromatic alteration* of specific pitches may arise because of ascending/descending scale forms, raised leading tones or subtonics, and idiomatic, idiosyncratic alterations for color.

Definitive *motives* and elastically conceived *themes* constitute another definitive feature of some maqam traditions. Some motives are three- or four-note gestures that immediately signal the identity of a maqam; many other motives are generic and found throughout a repertoire and define a traditional style in general. Final and (particularly) starting tones are often characterized by idiomatic motives, which may serve as an "upbeat" (comparable to the *initia* of Western plainsong) or decorate the duration of the tone. Themes may be present in the form of *cadential formulae* varying from a few notes to phrases lasting thirty seconds or more (particularly in Iran). As an extension of melodic progression, many

Ex. 1.1 Three essential tetrachords

Ex 1.2 Three essential maqam scales

Ex. 1.3 Tetrachords arising from octave species of Ajam

Ex. 1.4 Tetrachords arising from octave species of Rast

Ex. 1.5 Tetrachord arising from octave species of Hijaz

Ex. 1.6 Some common maqam scales and their component tetrachords

Segah scale

Segah

Iraq

Hozzam scale

Hijaz

Segah trichord

Rast trichord

Jahargah scale

Ajam

Rast

Ajam scale

Ajam

Ajam

Ex. 1.7 Common maqam scales arising from octave species of Rast

Husseini

Jahargah

Segah

Iraq

Nawa
(Persian and Iraqi)

Beyati

Octave species of Hijaz

Qarjigar

Nagriz

Suznak

Hozzam

Nahawand

Octave species of Ajam

(Panjgah?)

Nahawand

Kurd

Lami
(Iraqi)

maqams feature themes that may be expanded or contracted in performance or composition: for example, maqams Beyat and Hijaz feature a definitive descent from 4 to 1 which may appear in various guises.

Transposition is a fundamental modal process, already seen above with scale categorization, for which traditional practices vary widely. Unlike Western tonal music, transposition within the system is not exhaustive. Some transpositions are more idiomatic than others but it is difficult to discuss this in general terms without entering the complexities of individual traditions. Closely related to transposition, *modulation* is perhaps the most definitive feature of West Asian modes. Again, local practices vary widely and in this respect the traditions of Iraq and Iran represent the most rigid practice, Mashreqi Arab less rigid, and Turkish the most liberal. In some cases modulation may be the shift of melodic focus away from the tonic to another area of the same fundamental scale (particularly in Iran and Iraq). A more fundamental category of modulation is that which involves a change of scale type, normally occuring on idiomatic degrees of the original maqam. Many interesting common points of aesthetics and structure exist between West Asian and European conceptions of modulation; its skillful, creative, and resourceful use is a primary rhetorical device in both traditions. As Marcus noted (1992, 175), modulation is so central to maqams that, unlike Indian *ragas*, which may be studied in isolation, one cannot fully understand or appreciate an individual maqam outside its wider modulatory context. To know one you must know them all.[5] As with transposition, some modulations are more idiomatic than others; some are so common that they are by now prescriptions or clichés.

Compounding processes also figure into many traditions (particularly Turkish) wherein the melodic progression of a maqam is defined not only by contour, but also by a prescribed modulation. A compound maqam begins in a particular maqam and modulates midway to another, in which it ends; both component maqams receive equal weight. The combinatory possibilities of creating new maqams are thus immense. An abbreviated type of compounding occurs in maqams that feature the effect of a *deceptive cadence.* Here a particular mode is firmly established, only to end suprisingly with a quick cadential shift to an unexpected tonic (cf., Feldman 1996, 238–39), often a third below the previously established modality. Fred Stubbs suggested another more subtle form of compounding in Turkish makam (which could be applied to other traditions) involving an implied type of modal foil character within an individual basic makam, a subtly schizophrenic tension between its definitive identity and a contrasting pole that is usually in an octave species relationship (personal communication, 1992). Makam Rast, for example, often flirts with the edges of Uşşak, Bayati often implies Acem (on 6) or Nihavent (on 4), and so on.

As in all West Asian arts, *ornamentation* is integral to the performance of maqams. Traditions are quite varied in this respect and indeed may be identified by their particular idioms of ornamentation. Standard ornaments such as mordents, turns, and trills are common to all but there is a universe of others, particularly in vocal genres, including glottal techniques, various levels of vibrato, glissandi, figurations, and effects that involve acoustic noise. Most traditions also value extended *melismata*, which upon close examination vary considerably from one tradition to another. *Variation* and *development* of materials on all structural levels characterize maqam traditions, the effect of which may seem highly redundant upon initial listening. In general, more focus and value is placed upon eloquent and rhetorical delivery of conventionalized materials than upon the creation of novel structures.

Improvisation and *composition* straddle the borders of process and form; the emic West Asian conceptions of both are reasonably close to Western definitions. Bearing in mind the usual precautions when making sweeping generalizations, improvisation (beyond foreground ornamentation) tends to be ametrical and through-composed, while compositions are generally metrical and feature *return forms*, such as a rondolike refrain[6] with episodes or an ABA recapitulation. This latter ternary template is archetypal in both improvisational and compositional forms, as pieces generally begin in a "tonic" maqam, proceed through various modulations, and eventually return home. The midpoint or three-quarter point of this template often corresponds with the apogee and the most remote modulation of the piece. As mentioned earlier, *large cyclical forms* or suites, whose individual components may vary from short melodic fragments to long compositions in contrasting forms, characterize most maqam traditions. Some maqam traditions—Iran, Iraq, and Azerbaijan in particular—reflect the tune pole of Powers's continuum mentioned above and are organized as sets of melodies. Each set has a tonic modality and melodic theme under or around which various others congregate as satellites, and which may be termed generically as *submodes*. In some respects submodes correspond to the notion of closely related maqams or even compound maqams (as discussed above regarding modulation) but are differentiated, among other things, by featuring prescribed melodies and being ordered in a conventional manner, which also prescribes form to some extent. In these traditions a mode is partially defined by its collection of component submodes.

These are exceedingly complex and subtle concepts that fortunately have been explicated in detail by others for Iran, Azerbaijan, Turkey, and the Mashreq (see During 1984, 1988, 1991; Nettl 1992; Tala'i 2000; Zonis 1973; Feldman

1996; Signell 1977, 2002; d'Erlanger 1949; Marcus 1989, 2002). With this brief and general outline providing the larger context of maqam theory, we may now proceed to the particulars of Iraqi maqam.

The Basic Structures and Terminology of Iraqi Maqam

Cultural outsiders interested in understanding the musical structure of Iraqi maqam are confronted with a number of difficulties and potential confusions, largely because the use of terminology found in the better-known maqam cultures often acquires entirely different meanings in Iraq. Another problem is the bewildering number of unfamiliar proper names for modes[7] and their components, most of which largely correspond in some measure to standard scales and modes found elsewhere in West Asia. Their specific formulation and usage indicates that we must consider Iraq as a separate tradition. The subtle differences evident when scrutinizing seemingly identical materials (scales, progression, motives) through ornamentation, function, transposition, affixation, and other processes reflect similar dynamics in the grammar of the Arabic language, where trilateral roots are subject to variation procedures that create a rich array of semantic nuances.

Iraqi maqam features a satisfying balance and variety of form and melody (preset, improvised), rhythm (free, metric, or the superimposition of both), poetic text, and modal modulation. The scale and proportion of a maqam performance is well paced and easily digestible. While concise performances can be five minutes (e.g., early 78 recordings), more developed renditions evident on long-play recordings rarely exceed twenty minutes—this usually includes a *pesta* (strophic song) for a concluding section of five minutes or so. LP-era recordings generally average a total of fifteen minutes, which corresponds to Kojaman's description of *chalghi* evening performance durations (2001, 129). Improvisation concerns choices regarding the repetition of phrases, foreground decoration and variation, selection of optional components, idiosyncratic vocal techniques, and speed or tempo of delivery (Scheherazade Hassan 1987, 47; Kojaman 2001, 124–26, 143).[8]

As with Persian *avaz*, the primary focus for the local listener of Iraqi maqam is the poetry, which also controls much of the reciter's rhythmic delivery. There are three types of poetry found in the repertoire, two of which are differentiated by the type of Arabic employed. Approximately two-thirds of the maqams are set to *qasida*s in classical Arabic. While they are usually drawn from famous poets, some reciters composed their own lyrics (Abu-Haidar 1988, 132). Reciters are free to choose poems that they feel are suitable for a particular maqam and may even omit lines of the poem, provided that elisions do not interfere with semantic continuity. The other third of the repertoire consists of *muwwal*s in a colloquial Iraqi Arabic known as *zheiri*,[9] which is uninflected, mixes urban and rural dialects, and features a sophisticated play on the multiple meanings of individual words. Written editions now exist for some of this poetry, which was traditionally transmitted orally; reciters take great creative liberties with its delivery, such as extending or contracting syllables and changing words or entire lines. A relatively short poem may form the basis of a lengthy maqam due to the rhetorical repetition of individual lines or couplets.[10] The third type of poetry is reserved for the pesta repertoire, which is lighter and less intellectually rigorous than the previous poetic genres.

In addition to the poetic text there is a large repertoire of specific vocables, interjections, words, and short phrases (e.g., *Ah, Aman, Ya lil, Ya leili, Ya habib*, etc.) unconnected to the selected poem, known as alfaz. Specific alfaz are generally prescribed to particular components of a maqam, particularly the tahrir, qit'as, and teslim, and feature a surprising variety of languages: Arabic, Turkish, Persian, and less frequently Kurdish or Hebrew. As mentioned above, Sha'oubi Ibrahim was forced by his nationalistic government employers to replace foreign words with Arabic ones (Kojaman 2001, 162–63). The tradition of Iraqi maqam is also defined by specific, virtuoso vocal techniques including a wide range of articulations (initial attacks, connecting or detaching notes, particularly abrupt stops or interruptions within a phrase) glottal ornaments similar to the Persian-Azeri *tekye*, scoops and glissandi, extended melismata, and various gradations of vibrato. Any precise description of these essential techniques and their resulting sound lies beyond the capabilites of written media.

Components

Most Iraqi authorities agree that individual Iraqi maqams consist of a maximum of six structural components: tahrir or bedwa, qit'a, qarar, jalsa, meyana, and teslim. Tahrir, qit'a, and meyana are thematic sections, while jalsa, teslim, and (usually) the qarar are cadential. Only six maqams in the repertoire feature all six components; the minimum number of components (according to H. Rijab 1983, 65) is three: tahrir/bedwa, qit'a, and teslim.[11] While the six components also constitute the main form of a maqam, Warkov (1986, 64–66) and Kojaman (1978) add the formal division of a central section/*matn* to describe the material between the tahrir and meyana, which often consolidates a succession of qit'as and the jalsa. One could also add instrumental sections of the introductory *dulab* or *moqadamme*, the preset refrain (in rhythmic maqams), and the improvised responsorial sections (*muhasiba*). Pestas are precomposed strophic songs to end the maqam on a light note; they are performed antiphonally rather than solo, allowing the reciter to rest while the accompanists and (in the traditional context of the coffeehouse or private gathering) the audience to sing. Abu-Haidar (1988, 132) describes pestas as "ditties," which is understandable but somewhat misleading, as some carry an intense expressive depth. There are some correspondences between this functional melodic compartmentalization and bardic narrative processes: the maqam is here analogous to the story, the components to the succession of the episodes, sub-plots, and links that propel the larger narrative. This accounts for various performance options, abbreviated or extended development, and the independent maqam status that some episodes may acquire. As experienced maqamists already know the story and punch line, the essence of maqam is in its delivery and animation. The bardic analogy could equally apply to the Persian radif and, in varying degrees, other maqam traditions.

In terms of the background structure, the overall form of a typical maqam is essentially tahrir/bedwa, central section, meyana, and teslim; these sections are often deliniated by the appearance of a jalsa or qarar. We will examine now these components individually, leaving the complex notion of qit'a for a more detailed discussion following this section.[12]

Tahrir/bedwa, jalsa, qarar, meyana, teslim

After a short composed instrumental introduction (*moqadamme*) drawn freely from a standard repertoire that includes exclusively Iraqi compositions, well-known Mashreqi *dulab*s, and excerpts from famous compositions in *sama'i* form, the solo exposition of a maqam begins with the *tahrir*. Not to be confused with the Persian reference to extended melismata, it is analogous in function to the Persian *daramad* (as Tsuge [1972] rightly noted), in which the main modality and character of the maqam/dastgah is established. H. Rijab (1983, 65) describes two kinds of *bedwa* ("entrance"[13]): long types (e.g., in maqam Nahawand) are known as tahrirs, and short ones (e.g., maqam Nari) as bedwa. According to Hamid al-Saadi, bedwa refers to a tahrir that begins in the high register (Kojaman 2001, 86). As mentioned above, the Iraqi tahrir is usually sung to prescribed alfaz; the same melody may be repeated or varied using poetry. In either case the emphasis is on extended vowel sounds. The tahrirs of many important maqams show a similar descending arch profile centered on either the tonic or most emphasized pitch and consisting of largely stepwise motion (**ex. 1.8**). This apparent regularity seems to highlight the modal parameters of scale and pitch hierarchy; most of these regular type tahrirs begin and end on the same pitch. Tahrirs do not necessarily end on the finalis or tonic of the maqam (e.g., Husseini, Beyat, Dasht).

Jalsa is a cadential formula that descends to the tonic and prepares the listener for the meyana that directly follows it. H. Rijab (1983, 67) distinguishes two kinds of jalsas: one that descends less than seven notes to the qarar (e.g., Rast, from B♭ or C), the other descends eight notes to the lower octave tonic (e.g., Ajam, Husseini). Descents are usually stepwise and often in long notes of more or less equal duration. Material of the jalsa is often identical to that of the teslim.

Qarar marks the descent to the lowest note of the performance, which is not necessarily the tonic, particularly in the 'Usheiran maqams—Ajam 'Usheiran, Husseini 'Usheiran, 'Araibun 'Usheiran. It is normally placed in the middle of the maqam, giving the reciter a brief moment of relaxation while providing the listener with a premonition of the teslim (H. Rijab 1983, 73).

The use of the term *meyana* in Iraq is similar to that of Turkey: a central contrasting section of a composition that shifts to a higher register and often modulates to a different mode. Meyanas for each maqam are prescribed melodic profiles and function in the same way as qit'as, of which they could be viewed as a subset; a particular maqam may have more than one meyana. Alternate takes of Yusuf Omar performing the same maqam show that meyanas can be open to considerable freedom regarding foreground decoration and extensions and varying repetitions of the basic phrase. There

Ex. 1.8 Archetypal Tahrir Profile

Sha'oubi Ibrahim
(1982)

Husseini

Ajam

Nawa

Segah

Beyat

Mansuri

Saba

Dasht

Awj

is also strict repetition of meyana materials both within the same performance and between different maqams. Although the meyana is an important and definitive component of Iraqi maqam, not all maqams have them. Their conspicuous absence particularly characterizes new maqams, notably those derived from qit'as expanded into maqams. In addition to the basic (*asliya*) maqams (Rast, Beyat, Hijaz Diwan, Segah, Husseini, Nawa, Ajam, Saba), the following maqams include meyanas: Mansuri, Taher, Awj, Khanabat, Awshar, Dashti, Panjgah, and Hijaz Shaytani (H. Rijab 1983, 69). The term *sayha* ("shout") denotes a particular style of singing in a high register characterized by a declamatory vocal technique; despite its apparent similarity, it is not considered a meyana (H. Rijab 1983, 69). Hamid al Saadi associates the term sayha with zheiri maqams that have no jalsa, wherein it replaces the meyana (Kojaman 2001, 187). H. Rijab (1983, 69) further distinguishes three types of meyanas based on their position in the maqam: following the jalsa in the first quarter of the maqam (as in maqams Beyat, Rast, Segah, Hijaz Diwan, Nawa, Mansuri, and Taher); following the jalsa in the middle or near the end of the maqam (Husseini, Saba, Ajam, Hijaz Shaytani); and optional placement anywhere in the maqam, although usually in the middle (Khanabat, Awj, Awshar, and Dashti).

Teslim is a descending melodic formula that returns the melodic focus to the tonic register (or lower in some maqams) and ends the maqam; it is often identical to the jalsa of the maqam (e.g., maqams Segah, Rast). As Tsuge noted (1972), it is analogous to the Persian *forud*; likewise there are also other cadential patterns that recur throughout the maqam (cf., long and short types of *forud*s).

Qit'a

Qit'a ("piece") is the most important structural concept for understanding Iraqi maqam and the most immediate and practical unit for the performer. It is also the most complex, multifaceted, and potentially baffling concept for the cultural outsider to grasp. In Iraq the terms *wasla* and *gufte* are synonymous with qit'a but used less frequently; the concept was called *shu'ab* in the nineteenth century (Abu-Haidar 1988, 129), a term signifying submode that dates back to the thirteenth-century Systematist school but which is still current in contemporary Azeri and Central Asian maqam cultures.

H. Rijab (1983, 71) notes four functions of the qit'a: to provide melodic variety, thereby relieving potential monotony; as a bridge to effect smooth modulation; to prepare the listener for the gradual rise in pitch during the course of the performance; and to prepare listeners for the eventual descent in pitch. Very generally, a qit'a is analogous in function, application and nature to the Persian gusheh (a short melodic composition that constitutes one component of a larger form, the dastgah); it is identified with a proper name; and it appears in a more or less set order within a given maqam. As with other comparative instances throughout this study, I draw on this analogy here to facilitate discussion, as the concept of the gusheh is accessible and clearly described in the literature (e.g., Zonis 1973, During 1984, Farhat 1991, Nettl 1992). Unlike gushehs, however, qit'as often include prescribed alfaz.

There seems to be three basic meanings for the term qit'a: 1) a section or subsection of a maqam in general, excluding the standard components of tahrir, teslim, and so on; 2) transpositions and repetitions of tahrirs or main themes from other maqams—designated here as type I qit'a (or qit'a I); and 3) a separate repertoire of specific melodic formulae, some with prescribed alfaz, each identified with a proper name—designated type II qit'as (qit'a II) throughout this study.

The first meaning allows for modulations to other modes without melodic prescriptions or proper names (simply "qit'a in *jins* [tetrachord] Rast"); this is a recent analytical/descriptive feature, propagated by Sha'oubi and others, that deliberately draws upon practices of Mashreqi and Turkish music (Scheherazade Hassan 1992, 264). One wonders how a traditional reciter would describe or identify these sections. The second and third meanings reflect the practices of Persian music, selecting from an ordered repertoire of preset melodic formulae. While Iraqi maqams are closely aligned to Persian practices, they are essentially of a hybrid nature, simultaneously representing the two poles of the archetypal continuum of tune and scale as described by Powers (1980, 377, 422ff). Like Persian gushehs, qit'as are hierarchical: some are mandatory, others are optional, and they generally follow a prescribed order of performance within the maqam. While some qit'as seem to allow for melodic freedom within a modulation (basic meaning no. 1 mentioned above), the mode to which the modulation is effected is prescribed. The tradition allows for some personal innovations by master performers, such as the inclusion of a new qit'a or the adaptation of an entire maqam (Scheherazade Hassan 1987, 47–49). The modal qualities of qit'as I and II are reinforced by shifting drones, a practice not exclusive to Iraqi maqam in

West Asia but one effectively and regularly exploited there; the progression of drones can have a vaguely contrapuntal effect in some maqams.

Like the gusheh, a qit'a is essentially an abstract model that exists in variant but explicit personal versions of masters; conservative and neophyte performers will follow these models closely. Capable artists may decorate the form within rather narrow limits during a performance. Comparatively speaking, qit'as are shorter than gushehs on average; many are short phrases (comparable to gushehs such as Muhayer and Morabad in the radif) and some mere motives (e.g., Iraqi Segah Halab, Buselik); they can be easily missed in performance. By contrast, Qazaz is one of the longest qit'as (although still much shorter than a parallel long gusheh in the radif) with two clearly differentiated themes. A qit'a is usually a phrase or two with little or no development other than the repetition of motives and short subphrases (cf., gusheh); short phrases are sometimes compounded into a longer string. While theoretically open to improvised development, Yusuf Omar's performances largely reflect the pedagogical models described in the sources, suggesting more a practice of repeating and ornamenting set material than freewheeling expansion. Some maqams (e.g., Segah, Ibrahimi) feature a rapid succession of short qit'as, while others expose, repeat, or develop one or two. Sometimes qit'as as performed by Sha'oubi Ibrahim will be abbreviated to a single gesture or even a single pitch (e.g., qit'a Hakimi in maqam Awj, 'Araibun Ajam in Qatar). Like gushehs, some qit'as can be transposed to different naghmahs while retaining their melodic identity: qit'as like Mthalatha seem to be transposable formulae in the generic mold of Persian *tekke* gushehs (Farhat 1991, 109–12). Transposed qit'as in maqams such as Arwah and Hakimi present some novel intervallic structures that privilege melodic line as their definitive characteristic. Others (such as Nahoft) vary their motivic content when transposed; a more significant variation of melodic shape occurs in Hijaz Madani when it is transposed (cf., maqams Rast, Hijaz Diwan, and Hijaz Shaytani).

The melodic profiles of qit'as seem equally divided between descending progressions (usually encompassing a fourth, less often a fifth or octave from first to last notes) and level or undulating contours that begin and end on the same pitch. Few ascend or present the ascending-descending progression common to Turkish and Persian music. Some qit'as seem to be close variants of each other and of maqam tahrirs—such as the groupings of Mukhalef Kirkuk/Mukhalef; Sunbule/Tiflis and other Segah meyanas, and Hijaz Achough/Shahnaz—and show affinities with the notion of gusheh group variation in Persian music (see Zonis 1973, 49; 120–25). There are several qit'as that are variants of the definitive 4-1 descent of Beyat.

Qit'a I, recycling, modulation and transposition

For lack of an indigenous term, I use "type I qit'a" or "qit'a I" to refer to the transposition of definitive material (the melody of the tahrir or the maqam's strophic theme) from one maqam that functions as a qit'a in another maqam; the recycled material can be transposed to a different pitch from its usual tonic. This practice is characteristic of the structure of Iraqi maqam, occurring with such frequency that it would seem to warrant a separate theoretical term. Type I qit'as are interesting examples of the hybrid nature of Iraqi maqam, suggesting both the Turkish-Mashreqi notion of modulation to a new mode (on perhaps a different tonic pitch) and the Persian practice of a prescribed melody. To further press the Persian "tune" analogy, the Iraqi practice corresponds to the principle of moving or transposing daramad material of a particular dastgah into a different dastgah, as occurs in gushehs such as Shekaste (which resembles the daramad of Afshari) in Mahur, Mukhalef in Chahargah (cf., daramad of Homayun), Mukhalef in Segah (cf., daramad of Esfahan), various manifestations of transposed Shur (e.g., 'Ushshaq, Delkash, Muye of Segah), and so on. Iraqi maqams also reflect nuances of the Turkish-Mashreqi practice, where transposed modes often acquire new names (e.g., in Turkey Buselik becomes Nihavent, Zirgüleli Hicaz becomes Hicazkar, Evcara, etc.), in which case the two scales usually have different melodic progressions or other modal features; in some cases they may be simply viewed as tetrachords transposed to different pitches (e.g., *cins* Hicaz on Neva/D). Many themes of independent maqams that are now largely obsolete remain in the repertoire as subordinate qit'as. According to H. Rijab (1983, 53) these include: Qariabash, Omar Gala, Mukhalef Kirkuk, Alizabar, Segah Ajam, Segah Balban; Sha'oubi (1982, 14) adds Mathnawi, Bashiri, Hijaz Achough, Dasht 'Arab, Qazaz, Hijaz Shaytani, Gulguli, Bajalan, Nawruz Ajam, Beyat Ajam, Tiflis, Jamal, and Sa'idi. While the performance of these as maqams is undoubtedly rare, it is difficult to ascertain whether they are indeed defunct—Hamid al-Saadi still performs at least the latter three maqams and has recorded Jamal and Sa'idi Mubarqa. One can only hope that contemporary reciters retain and reinvigorate this portion of the repertoire.

Themes of all basic maqams function as type I qit'as—Beyat, Husseini, Saba, and Jahargah are the most common, judging from the comprehensive listings of Sha'oubi. Nonbasic maqams appear with varying frequency, many in only one instance: Awshar, Gulguli, Jamal, Hijaz Shaytani, Hijaz Achough, Lami, Madmi, Mathnawi, Nahawand, Orfa, Panjgah, Rashdi, Sharqi Rast, and 'Ushshaq. The most frequently encountered qit'a I is Juburi, occuring in at least eight maqams, followed by Mahmudi and Qatar (in five maqams). Type I qit'as occurring in two to four maqams include: Arwah, 'Araibun Ajam, Bheirzawi, Dasht, Hakimi, Ibrahimi, Mischin, Mugabl, Quriyat, Sa'idi, and Taher. B. Rijab mentions two other type I qit'as not included in the listings of Sha'oubi: Khalwati in maqams Husseini and Saba, and Bajalan in maqam Segah. An exceptional case of complicated transposition occurs with the qit'a Mukhalef of maqam Hijaz Kar and Arwah—while the same melodic shape is apparent, the intervallic structure of the qit'a is radically altered (see entries in the maqam anthology).

Qit'as are the means by which modulation is accomplished in Iraqi maqam. To conclude this section, **table 1.1** lists the sequence of modulations of naghmah in the order that they appear in basic maqams. "Saba/2" denotes a modulation to the maqam scale of Saba, built on the second degree of the original maqam. Qit'as that change their tune or polarize a different degree but remain within the original maqam scale are not included. Maqams in parentheses indicate a brief allusion to this naghmah. Iraqi modulation generally follows the conventional grammar of Mashreqi modulation as described by Marcus (1992) but there are exceptions that point to the freer practices of Turkish makam. In maqams Beyat and Nawa we find modulations to Rast and Jahargah on 7; maqam Rast Turki features Saba and Hijaz on 2. The preponderance of Saba throughout the repertoire reflects a similar prediliction in Turkish makam.

Table 1.1. Modulation of naghmah in the components of basic maqams

Beyat:	Jahargah/3, Saba/1, Rast/7, Ajam/6, Jahargah/3, Ajam/6, (Saba/1)
Husseini:	Rast/3, (Saba/1[14])
Nawa:	Beyat, Segah, Jahargah-Rast/7, (Saba/5)
Nahawand:	Beyat/5, Ajam/3
Rast Hindi:	Saba/5, Beyat/5, Hijaz/5, Segah /3', Jahargah/4', Rast/8, Hijaz/5
Rast Turki:	(Saba/2), Hijaz/2
Hijaz Diwan:	Husseini/5, Rast/4, Beyat/8, Saba/8, Beyat/8, Saba/8
Saba:	Segah/<u>6</u>[15], Beyat/1, Jahargah/3
Mansuri:	Saba-Beyat compound/1, Husseini/1, Hijaz/1, Husseini/1, Beyat/1
Ajam:	Beyat/3, Saba/<u>6</u>
Jahargah:	Saba/6
Segah:	Saba/3, Mukhalef/8, Hijaz/3

Listings and profiles of type II qit'as

Type II qit'as form a repertoire of submodes in the tradition of Iraqi maqam. The number of canonic type II qit'as is roughly forty: B. Rijab (1985, 18–32) lists thirt-two, Sha'oubi (1982, 14) lists only twenty-eight but actually presents at least thirty-seven. Assembling a precise, complete roster is both impossible and futile, as the repertoire of both qit'as and maqams is in a constant flux—old pieces become obsolete as new ones are created. Based on the consensus of authoritative sources, however, the following seem to constitute a core repertoire (**table 1.2**):

Table 1. 2. Type II Qit'as

Aboush	Kuyani	Qatuli	Sisani
Aidin	Lawouk	Qazaz	Sunbule
'Ardhibar/'Alizabar	Mahuri	Quriyat	Sufyan
Bakhtiar	Mukhalef Kirkuk	Rukbani	'Udhdhal
Buselik	Muste'ar	Salmak	'Ushaish
Hijaz Gharib	Nagriz	Segah Ajam	'Ushshaq
Hijaz Madani (3 versions)	Nahoft (3 versions)	Segah Balban	Yatimi
Iraq	'Omar Gala	Segah Halab	Zanburi
Jasas	Qaderbijan	Sereng/Mthalatha	Zaza
Khalili	Qariabash	Shahnaz	

The most widely distributed type II qit'as throughout the repertoire are Mukhalef Kirkuk (found in six maqams in Sha'oubi [1982]), followed by Hijaz Gharib and Mthalatha (five maqams each). Qit'as found in three or four maqams include Aboush, 'Omar Gala, 'Ushaish, Aidin, Khalili, and Qariabash. Qit'as more restricted in use and distribution than the above, only appearing in one or two maqams include Rukbani, Kuyani, 'Ushshaq, Zaza, Salmak, Sunbule, Nagriz, Jasas, Lawouk, Muste'ar, Qazaz, Sufyan, Segah Balban, and 'Udhdhal.

As is common in maqam cultures, in Iraq the proper names of qit'as and maqams derive from a variety of sources, often extramusical: geography (e.g., Orfa [Turkey], Segah Halab [Aleppo], Hijaz [Western Saudi Arabia]); ethnic groups (Beyat, Juburi, Kurd); individual people (Husseini, 'Omar Gala, Hakimi); music theory, usually a pitch or tetrachord name (Segah, Husseini, Nawa); poetic forms (Mathnawi, Lawouk) or idioms (Saba); and Sufism (Khalwati, 'Ushshaq, Nahoft). The nomenclature serves as a fascinating collection of local histories or bardic components that form the "epic" of the Iraqi maqam tradition.

Like early radif sources, many Iraqi publications list and discuss qit'as without providing a clear, detailed insight into their musical structure. Fortunate exceptions include B. Rijab, who begins his study with transcriptions of idealized models (1985, 22–32), and Sha'oubi (1982), who identifies qit'as in his recording by citing their corresponding poetic text; Scheherazade Hassan (1995a) also identifies qit'as in Yusuf Omar's recordings by their corresponding text and ordinal sequence. In the vast majority of cases these sources are consistent with regard to the musical contents of qit'as, providing us with a reasonably clear and reliable description of each. **Ex. 1.9** provides an outline for each qit'a (based largely on abstractions of transcriptions from B. Rijab, a few are from Sha'oubi's recordings); a list of maqams in which it appears, its prescribed alfaz, if applicable,[16] and distribution in the repertoire. Qit'as in the list are grouped by naghmah and respective maqam tonic family. These transcriptions are rather abstract and the reader is encouraged to refer to performance renditions transcribed in the following anthology. The largest modal family of qit'as is Segah, followed by Beyat; there are relatively few in Rast, Hijaz, and Jahargah (Saba appears only as a passing allusion). A separate listing is given for qit'as that are frequently transposed. Some qit'as feature a brief allusion to another mode within its main modality, others have a compound mode structure (the qit'a is then arbitrarily listed under its concluding maqam: e.g., Yatimi is a Rast/Nahawand compound and is filed under Nahawand). Other than identifying their naghmahs, the musical contents of the following rare type II qit'as listed by Hamid al-Saadi (in Kojaman 2001, 171–76) are not known: Abu Ata (naghmah Husseini), Humaydiyya (Beyat), Jannazi (Saba), Mo'at al-Nawa (Nahawand), and Zanganai (Jahargah).

To summarize this section, the main melodic components of an Iraqi maqam are prescribed themes and formulae with various functions and modulation schemes, their ordering and rendering in performance creates formal sections: the definitive tahrir and the main thematic material of the maqam; a repertoire of ordered themes—type I qit'as (transpositions of tahrirs or definitive themes from other maqams), type II qit'as (prescribed, independent melodies); most maqams include one or more meyanas (climaxes); and jalsa and teslim cadences. The form of the maqam itself is framed by an instrumental introduction and a concluding pesta. A schematic representation of a typical, complete maqam performance follows:

Instrumental Introduction	Tahrir	"theme" of maqam	Qit'a or group of qit'as	Jalsa	Instr. interlude	Meyana (1 or more)	Qit'a/s	Teslim	Pesta (strophic)
Iqa'		Unaccompanied or with iqa' and refrain			(some maqams feature a change of iqa')				New Iqa'

Ex. 1.9 Qit'a II Profiles, Alfaz, Distribution

(adapted from B. Rijab 1985, 22ff)

Naghmah Rast

Khalili: *Nazaniniman*; maqams Rashdi, Rast, Taher

Mahuri: maqams Jahargah, Khalwati, Taher

Sisani: *Ah ya*; maqams Bajalan, Hleilawi

Zanburi: maqams Ibrahimi, Mukhalef

Naghmah Nahawand

Buselik: *Janajanem wa*; maqams Hijaz Diwan, Husseini

Yatimi: maqams Khanabat, Quriyat

(Yatimi cont'd)

Naghmah Nagriz

Aidin: *Ah*; maqams Mahmudi, Mischin, Rashdi, Taher

Naghmah Hijaz

Segah Halab: *Aman*; maqam Segah

Shahnaz: *Ah ya leili* in Hijaz Diwan; *Aw wai* in 'Araibun Ajam

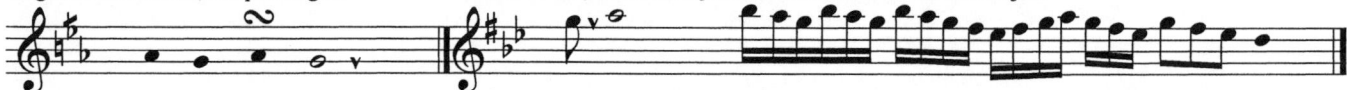

Naghmah Beyat

Aboush: *Ah*; maqams Hadidi, Ibrahimi, Mahmudi, Mansuri, Mugabl, Mukhalef, Saba

'Ardhibar/'Alizabar: *Ah* in Dasht 'Arab, *Deyi* in Ibrahimi, *Hanin yaba* in Mahmudi

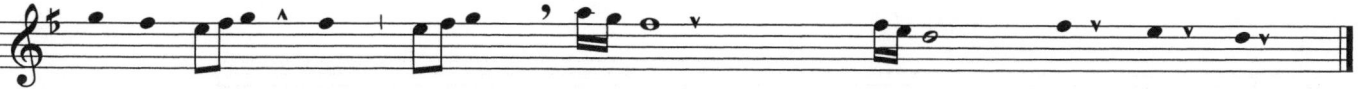

Hijaz Gharib: *Ay dad bidam;* in maqams Mansuri, Mukhalef (N.B., in other contexts this is a type I qit'a in naghmah Hijaz)

'Omar Gala: *La welak/Alilu*; maqams Bheirzawi, Hadidi, Ibrahimi, Juburi, Mahmudi, Mugabl, Quriyat

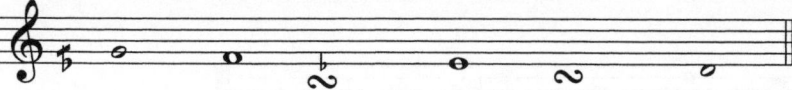

Qariabash: *Babam qurban hayran aki gozem*; maqams Bheirzawi, Hadidi, Beyat, Juburi, Mahmudi, Mugabl

Qazaz: *Man aman*; maqams Homayun, Hijaz Diwan, Huizawi, Ibrahimi, Jamal, Mathnawi

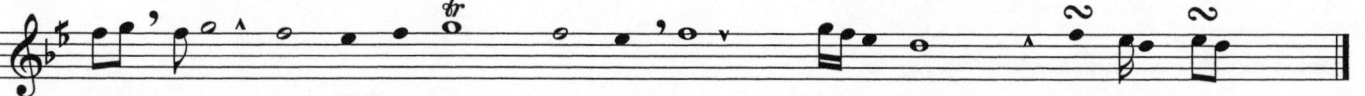

'Ushaish: *Weyay akh akh;* maqams Ajam, Arwah, Nawa, Orfa, Sharqi Dogah

   (in maqam Nawa)   (in maqam Orfa)

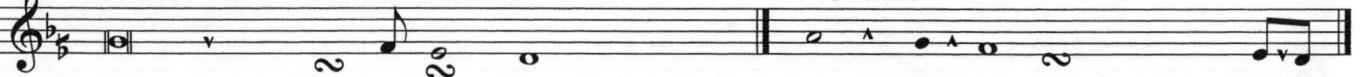

Naghmahs Segah, Hozzam, and Mukhalef

Bakhtiar: *Aman deli bidadam*; maqams Dasht 'Arab, Khanabat

Jasas: *Ah*; maqam Segah

Kuyani: *Yab yayab cham yayab ah*; maqam Mukhalef

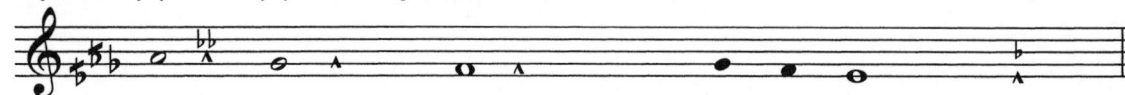

Mukhalef Kirkuk: *Yaya yay ay*; maqams Arwah, Awj, Hakimi, Hijaz Kar, Hleilawi, Huizawi, Mukhalef, Segah, Tiflis

Muste'ar: maqams Awj, Hijaz Kar

'Udhdhal: *Leil*; maqam Mukhalef

Qaderbijan: *Ya dost/Aman*; maqams Awj, Hakimi

Qatuli: maqam Mukhalef

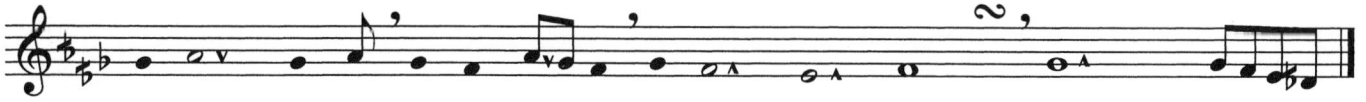

Rukbani: maqam Hakimi (from Sha'oubi Ibrahim 1982)

Salmak: maqam Segah (B. Rijab 1985, 67)

Segah Ajam: *Dad bidad*; maqam Segah

Segah Balban: *Yadost aman*; maqams Jamal, Rast, Segah

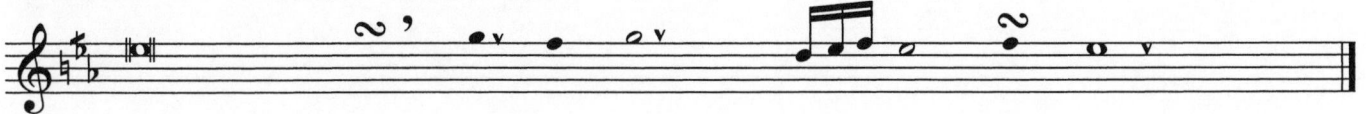

Sufyan: *Yaba dakhl aman*; maqams 'Araibun 'Arab, Awj, Nari, Segah, Tiflis

Sunbule: *Mana la welak la*; maqams Ibrahimi, Juburi, Segah (B. Rijab 1985, 67)

(another version of Sunbule from maqam Segah)

Naghmah Jahargah

Lawouk: *Yay away*; maqams Beyat (two versions), Orfa

Lawouk I (in maqam Beyat)

Lawouk II

(in maqam Orfa)

Naghmah Husseini

Zaza: *Lilay way delay yay*; maqams Orfa, Sharqi Dogah (from Sha'oubi Ibrahim 1982)

Transposing Qit'as

Hijaz Madani: *Faryademan ya dost madad aman* in maqam Rast

Aw in maqam Hijaz Diwan

Badustam aman in maqam Hijaz Shaytani

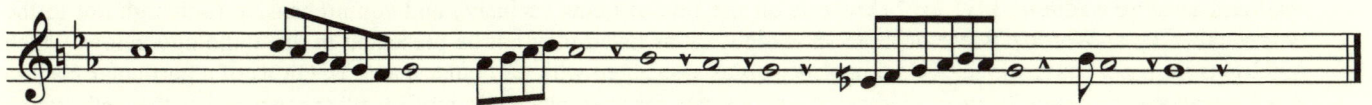

Mthalatha/Sereng: maqams Bajalan, Beyat, Bheirzawi, Hadidi, Hijaz Shaytani, Hleilawi, Husseini, Ibrahimi, Juburi, Kurd, Mischin, Mahmudi, Mansuri, Mugabl, Nahawand, Nari, Qatar, Rashdi, Segah, Orfa

(in maqam Segah)

(in Mansuri)

Nahoft: *Ah akh*

(in maqam Beyat)

(in Mansuri)

(in Segah)

Maqam

Repertoire and components

The total number of maqams currently in the Baghdadi repertoire numbers around fifty but some estimates exceed sixty (Warkov 1987, 70n26). Again, due to historical flux it is both impossible and pointless to establish their exact number or compile a roster that is completely consistent with the available sources (cf., Marcus 2002, 43). What emerges from the sources, however, is a reasonably reliable outline of the most important, or at least current, repertoire of the period. **Table 1.3** lists forty-seven maqams along with their constituent qit'as, based on the consolidated listings of Sha'oubi (1982), H. Rijab (1983), B. Rijab (1985), Hamid al-Saadi (in Kojaman 2001), and occasionally al-Amiri (1990). The latter three sources are abbreviated HR, BR, HS, and TA respectively to indicate specific designations in the table when listings lie outside a larger consensus. Al-Wardi's study of maqam Mukhalef illustrates well the futility of establishing a definitive list of qit'as—performances by sixteen reciters yielded some twenty-five different qit'as (1969, 44), six of the qit'as were widely distributed, while most of the others were only present in a single performance. This is indicative of a vital and creative tradition. My list below errs on the side of being inclusive and comprehensive (although not to the degree taken by al-Wardi!). Some of these anomolous qit'as listed may not be presented in the anthology below, which highlights the most conventional and compulsory qit'as associated with particular maqams. Qit'as of a particular maqam that have alternate nomenclature are indicated with a slash: for example, "Mischin/Beyat" are two names that refer to the same musical material in this particular maqam.

The greater number of type I qit'as over type II is striking. Excluding parenthetical listings of a single qit'a, fifteen maqams have no type II qit'as at all, a characteristic feature of newer maqams based on qit'a expansions; these maqams usually lack meyanas as well. Many maqams on the list appear to be rare within the repertoire that was current in the 1970s: Beyat Ajam, Mathnawi, and Sa'idi show similar contents, specifically the type I qit'as of 'Araibun Ajam, Huizawi, Khanabat, and Madmi. Lists of Wardi (in Tsuge 1972 and Moussali 1995) reveal a number of yet more obscure, probably defunct, maqams.[17] The fact that most of these obscure maqams, which amount to about one-fifth of the total repertoire, exist as type I qit'as in other current maqams illustrates an essential ambiguity of the hierarchy, and likely reflects the flux of material through recent history. Similar ambiguities exist in Persian music—the quasi-independent gushehs such as Bayat-e Kord, Mukhalef-e Segah, and Shushtari—but on a smaller scale. Ambiguous qit'a/maqams of this type include Mathnawi, Lami, Bajalan, 'Araibun Arab, Khaburi, Khalwati, Quriyat, Nawruz Ajam, 'Ushshaq, Beyat Ajam, Tiflis, Jamal, Gulguli, Bashiri, Bakhtiar, Hijaz Shaytani, Hijaz Achough, Hijaz Gharib, Mukhalef Kirkuk, Qariabash, and Sa'idi. These maqams are either unlisted or got one or two performances in Warkov's list of performances by four prominent reciters on Israeli radio in the period preceding 1981 (Khalwati and Jamal tallied three each) (1987, 247).

In contrast to the large catalogs of neglected modal inventions in Turkish and North Indian traditions, there are a number of such recent creations current in the Iraqi canon. Part of the reason why the Iraqi tradition is a nexus of the surrounding maqam cultures is due to its geographic centrality and the deliberate importation and adaptation of modes from Iran and the Mashreq. According to 'Abd al-Wahhab Bilal (cited in Warkov 1987, 71–73) and Kojaman (2001, 136), Mohammed Qubanchi composed or arranged maqams Lami, Qatar, Homayun (imported from Iran), Hijaz Kar, Kurd, and Nahawand (the latter three imported from the Mashreq). It is interesting to note how these recent importations are integrated into older standard maqams as type I qit'as. Some reciters and maqam enthusiasts rejected Qubanchi's innovations dating from the 1930s, placing them outside the Baghdadi tradition (Kojaman 2001, 141). Qubanchi was clearly following the traditional creative practices of his (and Qundarchi's) master Ahmad Zaydan (1829–1912), who created maqams Mischin, Qariabash, and 'Omar Gala by adding components to these qit'as (the latter two maqams are no longer current), and imported Dasht from Iran.[18] Other relatively recent qit'a expansions include maqam Tiflis (credited to Zaydan's master, Rahmat Allah Shaltagh [d. 1871]), Mahmudi (anonymously), and Qazaz (by 'Izzat al-Masaraf; no longer current as a maqam but remains as a qit'a). Kojaman notes that this twentieth-century increase in maqams is quantitative and not qualitative (1978, 64). As mentioned above, these new maqams generally lack meyanas, are more restricted in modulation, and include much less, if any, of the separate qit'a II repertoire; they are shorter and less complex than the rest of the repertoire.

Table 1.3. Maqams with qit'a components

Maqam	Type I qit'as	Type II qit'as
Ajam	Meyana Beyat, Saba, (HS: Jahargah)	(HS: 'Ushaish)
'Araibun Ajam	Sa'idi, Segah, Qatar, Ibrahimi, Bheirzawi, 'Araibun Arab, (HS: Hijaz Diwan)	(HS: Shahnaz, Sufyan)
'Araibun Arab (HS)	Bheirzawi, Mahmudi, Quriyat	Sereng
Arwah	Mukhalef, Husseini, Juburi, Hijaz Gharib, Dashti, Taher, (HS: Jahargah, Orfa)	'Ushaish, Kuyani, (HS: Abu Ata; BR: Mukhalef Kirkuk)
Awj	Hakimi, (HS: Mukhalef)	Sufyan, Muste'ar, Mukhalef Kirkuk, 'Ushshaq, Qaderbijan, Arwah
Awshar	Mansuri, (HS: Mukhalef)	
Bajalan (HS)	Hijaz Shaytani, Qatar, (HR: Hleilawi; TA: Huizawi, Mathnawi, 'Araibun Ajam)	Mthalatha, Sisani
Beyat	Nawa, Ajam, (BR: Saba)	Lawouk, Nahoft (HS: Mthalatha, Qariabash)
Beyat Ajam (HR)	Huizawi, 'Araibun Ajam, Madmi	
Bheirzawi	Mugabl, Juburi, Quriyat, Mahmudi, Jahargah, Rast/Mischin, Qatar, (HS: Ibrahimi, Khanabat)	Qariabash, Aboush, (HS: Mthalatha, 'Omar Gala)
Dasht	Lami, Husseini, Beyat, Hijaz Gharib, (HS: Hijaz Diwan)	(HS: Abu Ata)
Hadidi	Mahmudi, Mugabl, Madmi, (HS: Mansuri)	Aboush, 'Omar Gala, Qariabash, Iraq,[19] Mthalatha
Hakimi	Mukhalef, (HS: Mugabl)	Mukhalef Kirkuk, Qaderbijan, Rukbani
Hijaz Diwan	Husseini, Saba, Hijaz Achough (BR: Hijaz Shaytani; HS: Dashti, Mathnawi, Ibrahimi)	Nagriz, Qazaz, (BR: Hijaz Madani, Buselik, Shahnaz; HS: Jannazi)
Hijaz Kar	Hakimi, Mukhalef, (HS: Mugabl)	Mukhalef Kirkuk, Muste'ar
Hleilawi	(HS: Homayun, Nari, Qatar)	Mukhalef Kirkuk, Sisani, (HS: Mthalatha, Tiflis)
Homayun	Hijaz Diwan, Beyat, Hijaz Gharib, (HS: Huizawi)	(HS: Qazaz)
Huizawi	Sa'idi, Dashti, Hijaz Gharib, (HR: Madmi, Mathnawi, 'Araibun Ajam; HS: Lami, Nahawand)	(HS: Qazaz; BR: Mukhalef Kirkuk)
Husseini	Rast, Juburi/Beyat, (BR: Arwah, Khalwati; HS: Ibrahimi, Saba)	(BR: Buselik; HS: Mthalatha)

Ibrahimi	Jins Segah, jins Rast, Nari, "qarar Beyat," Taher, 'Araibun Ajam, Mahmudi, Mansuri, Quriyat, Qatar, Mugabl, Bheirzawi, Juburi, Mischin/Rast, (HS: Khanabat)	Sunbule, 'Omar Gala, Qariabash, Aboush, Zanburi, 'Ardhibar, (HS: Humaydiyya, Mthalatha/Sereng, Qazaz)
Jahargah	Saba, Taher, Rashdi	(HS: Abu Ata, Mahuri)
Jamal (HS)	Hijaz Diwan, Homayun, Huizawi	Qazaz, Segah Balban
Juburi	Mugabl, Qatar, Quriyat	Qariabash, 'Omar Gala, (HS: Humaydiyya, Mthalatha, Sunbule)
Khalwati (HR)	Saba, Taher, Ajam	
Khanabat	Nahawand, Dasht Arab, jins Beyat, (HS: Awshar, Mansuri)	Yatimi, Bakhtiari
Kurd	Beyat	(HS: Mthalatha)
Lami (TA)	Dashti, Husseini	Hijaz Gharib
Madmi	Sa'idi, 'Araibun Arab, Bheirzawi,[20] Hijaz Gharib (HS: Huizawi, Nahawand)	
Mahmudi	Juburi, Segah, Mugabl, Quriyat, Jahargah	Mthalatha, 'Omar Gala, Qariabash, Aidin, (HS: 'Alizabar; BR: Aboush)
Mansuri	Husseini and Rast meyanas, Mathnawi, Arwah, Beyat, (HS: Mukhalef, Saba; BR: Hijaz Gharib)	Nahoft, Mthalatha, (BR: Aboush)
Mathnawi (HR)	Huizawi, Madmi, 'Araibun Ajam, Khanabat, (HS: Homayun, Madmi; TA: Awj, Hakimi)	(HS: Qazaz; TA: Mukhalef Kirkuk)
Mischin	Mahmudi, jins Ajam, Beyat, Juburi, (HS: Mugabl)	Aidin, (HS: Mthalatha/Sereng)
Mugabl	Juburi, Quriyat, Qatar, Bheirzawi, 'Araibun Ajam, (HS: Madmi, Mischin)	(HS: Aboush, Mthalatha, Qariabash, 'Omar Gala)
Mukhalef	Mahmudi, Jahargah, Gulguli, (BR: Hijaz Gharib)	Mukhalef Kirkuk, Kuyani, 'Udhdhal, Qatuli, (HS: Aboush, Sereng, Zanburi)
Nahawand	Beyat, Nawa, Ajam Usheiran, (HS: 'Araibun Ajam)	(HS: Mthalatha)
Nari	Jins Segah, Beyat; Mukhalef, (HS: Quriyat)	Mthalatha, (HS: Sufyan)
Nawa	Ajam, Bayat, Juburi, jins Rast, Arwah, (BR: Mischin; HS: Mahmudi, Nahawand)	'Ushaish, (BR: Lawouk, Sunbule; HS: Mo'at al-Nawa, Sereng)
Orfa	Arwah/Beyat, Husseini, Dashti, Juburi, (HS: Hijaz Diwan, Lami, Mukhalef)	'Ushaish/Beyat, Zaza, (HS: Mthalatha; BR: Lawouk)
Panjgah	jins Hijaz, (HS: Mansuri, Mathnawi)	
Qatar	Homayun, 'Araibun Ajam	Mthalatha

Rashdi	Sharqi Rast, Saba, Jahargah, (HS: Bheirzawi, Nari, Taher)	Aidin, Khalili, (HS: Mthalatha)
Rast	Mansuri, Ibrahimi, Hijaz Shaytani, Mathnawi, (HS: Nari)	Khalili, Hijaz Madani, Nagriz, Segah Balban
Saba	Mahmudi, Awshar, Jahargah, (BR: Khalwati)	Aboush
Sa'idi (HR)	Mathnawi, Huizawi, Madmi, (HS: 'Araibun Ajam)	
Segah	Hakimi, Mukhalef, Tiflis, Jamal, (BR: Awshar, Bajalan; HS: Mansuri, Mugabl)	Jasas, Baste Negar, Segah Balban, Sufyan, Mthalatha, Mukhalef Kirkuk, Sunbule, (BR: Nahoft, Sereng, Segah Ajam)
Sharqi Dogah	Orfa, Arwah	'Ushaish, Zaza
SharqiRast/ Sharqi Esfahan	Qatar, Mischin, Panjgah, (HS: Mahmudi, Mukhalef, Taher)	
Taher	Mahmudi, Juburi, Jahargah, Husseini, Nawa, (HS: Arwah, Saba)	Aidin, Khalili, (HS: Mo'at al-Nawa, Zanganai; BR: Mahuri)
Tiflis (HR)	Awj, Hakimi	Mukhalef Kirkuk, Sufyan

Khaburi, like Rukbani (a qit'a in maqam Hakimi), is a genre of folk poetry and recitation of southern Iraq. Maqam Bashiri appears frequently in lists but is not described in sources, other than its membership to the Ajam family; H. Rijab (1983, 79) posits that this is because its prescribed text is in Turkish, which became politically unfashionable in recent decades (a similar situation exists for the maqams Bajalan and Tiflis[21]). Hamid al-Saadi has performed Bashiri and Tiflis with Arabic poetry, partially in an attempt to save them from extinction. Munir Bashir performed Bashiri on his last solo 'oud recording (Inedit W. 260050) but, aside from allusions to the tahrir contents, Bashir's renditions usually do not reflect the vocal tradition accurately enough for the purposes of this study.

The form and performance practice of individual Iraqi maqams are either "strict" or "free" (H. Rijab 1983, 36). In strict maqams (e.g., Nawa and Ibrahimi) all components and sections are followed in the order prescribed by tradition, although there are occasional options regarding the inclusion or exclusion of specific qit'as. Warkov reported that Iraqi émigrés in Israel rejected this practice, feeling that it was too rigid and inhibited individual creativity (1987, 63n12, 82). The ordering of components in free maqams (e.g., Awj, Madmi) is not prescribed, but rather performed at the reciter's discretion. From the cultural outsider's perspective, I perceive at least six overlapping types of maqams, three of which are types identified by H. Rijab:

1) "Big" maqams that contain a large number of qit'as include significant changes in modality (scale, range, polarized pitches, etc.), and have extended meyanas (e.g., Rast, Hijaz Diwan, Segah, Ibrahimi, Mansuri).

2) "Strophic" maqams that are characterized by a definitive theme which is repeated strophically throughout a large portion of the maqam (e.g., Husseini, Nawa, Mukhalef, Ajam, Saba).

3) "Simple" maqams that feature fewer qit'as, short meyanas, and are plainly structured as tahrir qit'a-meyana-teslim; they are often strophic and often lack meyanas or teslims (e.g., Homayun, Panjgah, Dasht, Orfa).

4) "Qit'a expansions" that are maqams with neither qit'as nor meyanas. Deriving from qit'as, they attain independent maqam status by the addition of a tahrir, jalsa, and teslim; they tend to be short in duration (e.g., Kurd, Sharqi Dogah). Recall that such change in status can flow in the other direction as well, where maqams can be subordinated to qit'as.

5) "Twin" maqams that are virtually identical, differing only in textual, rhythmical, and subtle melodic details, such as minor differences of range or delivery of text; they are considered to be interchangeable by some musicians (e.g., Bajalan/Hleilawi; Sa'idi/Mathnawi; Mukhalef/Gulguli; Hijaz Shaytani/Hijaz Achough; Rashdi/Bashiri).

6) Maqams with compound main themes (e.g., Husseini, Nawa, Mansuri) or closing gestures (e.g., Khanabat, Hleilawi, 'Araibun).

Maqam families

Like the Persian radif, the repertoire of Iraqi maqam is hierarchical. While there is traditionally a notion of seven basic (*asliyah*) maqams, the identity of a portion of this group is not entirely consistent in the sources. Rast, Beyat, Hijaz Diwan, and Segah form a consistent core while sources variously cite Jahargah, Ajam, Saba, Husseini, and Nawa as the remaining three basic maqams.[22] Qualification as a basic maqam often hinges on the choice of one from each of the following two pairs: Jahargah or Ajam, and Husseini or Nawa. The scalar structure of all basic maqams corresponds to that of identically named cognates in the Turkish-Mashreqi tradition. All of the other roughly forty maqams in the repertoire are considered to be derived (*far'iyya*) from the seven basic maqams. The derivation is largely based on shared scale, although there are other factors involved, judging from the list of maqam families in Sha'oubi (1982, 12–13). Reflecting the inconsistencies of individual opinions regarding maqam repertoire—a "wiggly" qualification that applies to virtually all maqam cultures—Sha'oubi presents not seven, as one might expect, but eleven families. The most notable organizational feature of Sha'oubi is his filing of Nawa (itself a borderline basic maqam) under a family for Nahawand—the latter is supposedly a modern maqam imported by Mohammed Qubanchi. The Jahargah/Ajam option falls in favor of Jahargah with Sha'oubi. Mukhalef, Hleilawi, and Kurd are considered as separate families: the former two are hybrid compound modes, and Kurd is another recent Qubanchi adaptation. A more complete listing follows (**table 1.4**), incorporating simple scalar affiliations and listings from other sources. Some maqams defy the linear rigidity of such classification: Mukhalef and Gulguli, the imported maqam Kurd, and the compound maqam Hleilawi lie outside the scheme. Kojaman (2001, 147-51) rightly notes that an empirical examination of the repertoire reveals a greater number of naghmahs than those of the seven basic maqams. The repertoire also includes Mukhalef and the Turkish-Mashreqi maqam scales of Kurd, Nahawand, Bastenegar, Hijaz Kar, Iraq, Nagriz, and Nawa'athar. But if we take into account the alternate basic families and recently (i.e., since the 1930s) imported or composed maqams (e.g., Nahawand, Kurd, Qatar, Lami, etc.), the traditional notion of seven scales appears to be a nineteenth-century concept that has become outdated.

Table 1.4 Maqam Families of the Baghdadi Repertoire

Naghmah/Family	Members
Beyat	Ibrahimi, Juburi, Mahmudi, Mugabl, Bheirzawi, Nari, 'Araibun Arab, Sharqi Dogah, Mischin, Nawruz Ajam, Quriyat
Rast	Panjgah, Sharqi Rast
Jahargah	(Ajam), Bashiri, Khalwati, Rashdi, Taher
Hijaz Diwan	'Araibun Ajam, Huizawi, Homayun, Qatar, Madmi, Hijaz Kar, Mathnawi, Sa'idi, Beyat Ajam, Hijaz Achough, Hijaz Shaytani
Saba	Mansuri, Hadidi
Husseini	Arwah, Orfa, Dasht
Segah	Awj, Awshar, Hakimi, Qazaz, Tiflis, Jamal, Bajalan
Nawa	Nahawand, Khanabat

While scale is perhaps the primary parameter of mode, pitch material of Iraqi maqam is largely aligned to the tune pole of the tune-scale continuum. This is clearly illustrated by the large Beyat and Hijaz families of maqams, the tahrirs and definitive phrases of which share the same scale and are largely differentiated by prescribed themes or tunes (see al-Basri 1996; and Elsner 1997 for an Algerian parallel). These tunes are fairly short, consisting of two to four phrases that are repeated and ornamented. Phrases of short Lutheran chorales can serve as a very rough cross-cultural analogy from Western music history regarding their length, character, and degree of fixity and flexibility. Signell has discussed how transposition affects the independence of a makam in Turkish music, where transposed scales (and tetrachords) may or may not acquire a new proper name from that of the parent makam (1977, 134ff). While certain melodic profiles create further ties between particular maqams,[23] the practice of transposition in type I qit'as allows for some freedom in this respect. Usually maqams within a family have clear and distinct melodic identities, even if they share a similar contour. There are other maqams aside from the Beyat and Hijaz families that feature this. Mansuri, for example, is distinguished from Saba by its transposition to G but more importantly by its melodic focus within the scale. I will restrict usage of maqam families throughout this study to the basic maqams (including Husseini, Nawa, and Jahargah). Recall that family members with similar tahrirs are also differentiated by text type, rhythmic accompaniment, and relative freedom in the content and ordering of qit'a components.

Rhythmic maqams

A large portion of the maqams in the repertoire are prescribed as "rhythmic" (*iqa'iya*)—partially or entirely accompanied by a rhythmic mode (iqa' or *wazn*, **ex. 1.10**). Important examples include maqams Segah, Husseini, Nawa, Mansuri, Mukhalef, Hakimi, Hadidi, Madmi, Sharqi Dogah, and Bheirzawi. Maqams that are accompanied rhythmically from beginning to end feature short refrains which begin the maqam and which are subsequently repeated between vocal sections, either replacing or tagged on to the end of the improvised solo responses. The rhythmic cycle may also change in the course of certain maqams (e.g., Segah, Nawa, and Mansuri, where the transition is from iqa' Samah to Yugrug). Some rhythmic maqams only introduce the iqa' in the first meyana, continuing to the teslim (e.g., Hijaz Diwan) or begin before the meyana and stop as the singing begins. While maqams Rast and Saba employ rhythmic cycles for prescribed instrumental interludes, all sung portions are in free meter. With the exception of Qatar and Hijaz Kar (recent additions to the repertoire), all maqams set to zheiri poetry are rhythmic. With the exception of iqa' Samah, the small repertoire of iqa's used in Iraqi maqam corresponds to those found in the larger rhythmic repertoire of the Mashreqi (particularly Syrian) *wasla* tradition. Jurjina originated in Iraq and accompanies many pestas but is rarely found in the body of a maqam itself (notable exceptions are maqams Hleilawi, Rashdi, and the more obscure Bajalan and Hijaz Shaytani). While the wonderful iqa' Ay Nawasi is regarded as being exclusively Iraqi, it does not appear in the maqam repertoire; Kojaman believes it was formerly used in maqams Ibrahimi and Nari (2001, 154–55).

The refrains appearing in Sha'oubi (1982), particularly those set in the iqa's Samah and Yugrug, are formulaic and can be viewed as generic themes or templates that are transposed to various maqam scales, affecting a unity within his presentation of the repertoire. These refrains in Yugrug (**ex. 1.11a**) consist largely of two such generic themes, arbitrarily labeled here as I and II. Contours of both are somewhat similar: I features an undulating 1-3-6̲-1; II is a more expansive 1-4/5/6-7̲-1. The last three beats may be left tacit, often serving as a dovetailing entrance point for the reciter, or feature a short "turnaround" gesture for repetitions. A similar tacit feature characterizes beats six to eight and the final three beats of the refrains in iqa' Samah (**ex. 1.11b**); these refrains have a wide currency among performers. Iqa's Wahda and Jurjina (**ex. 1.11c**) are less frequently used in rhythmic maqams and feature less melodic recycling. The tendency toward melodic recycling in refrains may be a characteristic of performances around the 1970s and '80s and particularly reflect Sha'oubi's tendency to simplify maqams. Earlier recordings show a much more diverse and complex approach to refrains, including varied sets of refrains within a single maqam, nonrecurring introductions, a thicker heterophonic texture, and shifts in tempo. These stylistic factors necessitate a tightly rehearsed ensemble or at least one consisting of musicians who have played together for a long period of time.

Ex. 1.10 Iqa' Repertoire

♩ = dum   ♩ = tek

Wahda

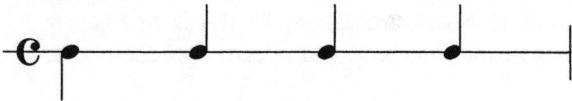

Sengin sama'i

Yugrug

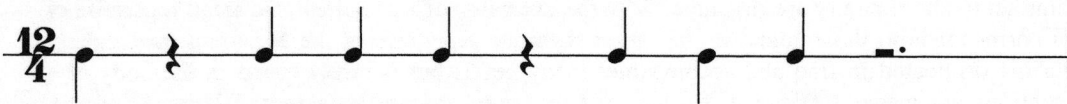

Jurjina

Samah

Ex. 1.11a Yugrug Refrains

Sha'oubi Ibrahim
(1982)

Generic Theme I

Jahargah and Taher

Khanabat

Madmi

Nari (the first note changes to G on repeat)

'Araibun

(fragment refrain)

Hakimi

Mukhalef

Generic Theme II

Mugabl

Juburi

Bheirzawi

Hadidi

(fragment refrain)

Ibrahimi

Ibrahimi in Yusuf Omar performance (al-Amiri 1990, 136)

Ex. 1.11b Maqams with combined Samah and Yugrug refrains

Samah

Mansuri

Segah

Nawa

Yugrug

Mansuri

Segah

Nawa

Ex. 1.11c   Wahda, Jurjina Refrains & Interludes

Iqa' Wahda

Sharqi Rast

Sharqi Dogah (Sha'oubi Ibrahim 1982)

Hijaz Diwan (begins before the meyana)

Saba interlude (B. Rijab 1985; begins after the jalsa)

Iqa' Wahda al-Maqsuma

Orfa (Sha'oubi Ibrahim 1982)

Arwah (Sha'oubi Ibrahim 1982)

Iqa' Jurjina

Rashdi (Sha'oubi Ibrahim 1982, 63)

"vamp"

Hleilawi (Sha'oubi Ibrahim 1982, 100)

"vamp"

(return to "vamp")

Other considerations

The collection of minor, generally newer maqams derived from expanding qit'as—ambiguously suspended between the two rubrics, as discussed above—form a subordinate subset of maqams. Furthermore, a basic distinction is made between secular and sacred recitation styles. Sacred style features a religious text, a freer and often abbreviated selection from the same melodic repertoire of themes and formulae used in secular recitation, and restricts instrumental accompaniment to the frame drum (see Kojaman 2001, 56–57, and the recording *Chants d'extase en Irak*, Al-Sur CD129).

Listeners can learn to identify maqams fairly readily by the following guidelines:
- What is the scale and melodic contour of the tahrir?
- What alfaz are used in the tahrir and teslim?
- Is it a rhythmic maqam, and if so, what is the iqa'?
- Readers familiar with Arabic poetry and dialects could ask: what type of poetry is employed?

This information is provided for each maqam in the anthology below.

Fasl

While no longer practically relevant in the second half of the twentieth century, about half of the repertoire was formerly organized and performed in five cycles, called *fusul* (sing. *fasl*); the Iraqi use of the term is similar to that of the Turkish tradition. A fasl was identified by the basic maqam that begins each group—Beyat, Hijaz Diwan, Rast, Nawa, or Husseini—and followed by four to seven various maqams in a prescribed order. Up to the mid-twentieth century, when small and intimate coffeehouses and private *chalghi* gatherings were the primary venue for the performance and transmission of Iraqi maqam, performing conventions took on marathon proportions. The practice seems to parallel those of epic recitation found throughout Asia. A reciter would sing continuously through an entire fasl (with only short, internal breaks provided by introductory instrumental compositions and pestas), take an intermission, and sing through subsequent fasls, covering virtually the entire repertoire (Kojaman 2001, 129ff). Kojaman (2001, 137) suggests that the fasl grew out of the *chalghi* context. Theoretically, a fasl such as Beyat or Husseini could last up to two hours, although renditions of some maqams were shorter and reciters could omit maqams in the fasl, providing the prescribed order (which is somewhat irregular in the sources) remained intact. With the decline of the all-night *chalghi* and the rise of the Pan-Arab style at the end of World War II, the fasl declined and musicians increasingly selected single maqams for performance. According to Abu-Haidar (1988, 130n17), non-fasl maqams would be performed as encores; Madmi and Bheirzawi are among the most important and popular of these.

Important fasl status is accorded to two maqams that are not clearly defined as being basic: Nawa and Husseini, as seen above, are often only alternately included. Some other maqams included in the fasl collection are largely obscure or even obsolete by now (Hijaz Shaytani, Quriyat, Beyat Ajam, Bajalan, and 'Ardhibar), illustrating the passing relevance of the fasl as an organizing unit. Nonetheless, aside from these the most important maqams in the repertoire are among the remaining twenty-four or so that are included within a fasl; non-fasl maqams are largely qit'a II derivations. It is interesting to note the ordering of Rast vs. Beyat: one would expect the tacit theoretical importance of Rast to precede Beyat.[24] From another perspective Rast is placed in the central position. **Table 1.5** provides a list of fasl collections, according to H. Rijab (1983). Kojaman (2001, 129–34) tabulates and discusses discrepencies of inclusion and ordering in various sources but privileges H. Rijab's listing. As with most attempts at establishing a definitive listing, one routinely encounters such variations, which reflect local and individual creative choices, and the richness and vitality of the tradition in general.

Table 1.5 Fasl Collections according to H. Rijab (1983, 100–02)

Fasl	Maqams included
Beyat	Beyat, Nari, Taher, Mahmudi, Segah, Mukhalef, Hleilawi
Hijaz	Hijaz Diwan, Quriyat, 'Araibun Ajam, 'Araibun Arab, Ibrahimi, Hadidi
Rast	Rast, Mansuri, Hijaz Shaytani, Juburi, Khanabat
Nawa	Nawa, Mischin, Ajam, Panjgah, Rashdi
Husseini	Husseini, Dasht, Orfa, Arwah, Awj, Hakimi, Saba

Just as most maqams present a progression of prescribed modulations, each fasl features a modulation scheme on a larger hierarchical level; **table 1.6** indicates the progression of naghmahs and the representative "family members." The relative infrequency of naghmah Rast is noteworthy, given the prominent status of maqam Rast in the repertoire.

Table 1.6. Scale Family Distribution in Fasls

Fasl	Naghmah	Maqam family members
Beyat	Beyat	Beyat, Nari
	Jahargah	Taher
	Beyat	Mahmudi
	Segah	Segah, (Bajalan)
	Mukhalef	Mukhalef
	Segah-Hijaz compound	Hleilawi
Hijaz	Hijaz	Hijaz Diwan
	Beyat	Quriyat
	Hijaz-Beyat compound	'Araibun Ajam, 'Araibun Arab
	Beyat	Ibrahimi
	Saba	Hadidi
Rast	Rast	Rast, (Sharqi Rast)
	Saba	Mansuri
	Hijaz	Hijaz Shaytani
	Beyat	Juburi
	Nahawand-Beyat compound	Khanabat
Nawa	Nawa	Nawa
	Beyat	Mischin
	Ajam	Ajam
	Rast	Panjgah
	Jahargah	Rashdi
Husseini	Husseini	Husseini, Dasht, Orfa, Arwah
	Segah	Awj, Hakimi
	Saba	Saba

The following figure summarizes the organization and hierarchy of the Iraqi maqam repertoire from the "top down" (i.e., reversing the order of their presentation in this introduction).[25]

BAGHDADI REPERTOIRE

> **5 Fasls**

> > **c. 50 Maqams**
> > 7 basic maqams
> > > c. 40 maqams with family affiliations
> > > c. 15 maqams derived from qit'as

> > > **Qit'as**
> > > qit'a I transpositions
> > > c. 40 qit'a II melodies

> > > > **Generic melodic fragments and motives**

Notes

1. A detailed discussion of how the materials here may be viewed as a paradigm of cognate modes must await a separate study.

2. But while the lower tetrachord name is Hijaz, in this instance the pitch Hijaz is not the tonic note, but rather the third degree; complexities and inconsistencies such as this characterize maqam theory in general.

3. The conception or generation of scales through octave species is indeed an old and widely distributed phenomenon found among the ancient Greek and Chinese modal systems, the Byzantine octoechoes modes, and the Indian concept of *murchana*.

4. It is important to remember that maqam traditions are not rigorously rational systems (e.g., like that of the Karnatak *melakarta ragas*) and not all permutations are used in actual practice. My priority here is to highlight the most fundamental structures; certain others are found but have a limited application in practice.

5. Or as Fred Stubbs once put it when referring to the Turkish tradition: "no makam is an island unto itself" (personal communication, 1992).

6. Improvisation based on the radif in Persian music also features this by successive returns to the daramad and forud patterns.

7. Some of these unfamiliar names were given wide exposure outside Iraq with Munir Bashir's solo recording of the early 1970s, *Iraq: 'ud classique arabe par Munir Bashir* (OCR 63). Jamil Bashir's recording from around the same period, *Luth traditionelle d'Iraq* (EMI Pathe 2C 0666-95160), while less famous than brother Munir's, featured more of this elusive repertoire.

8. While acknowledging these features Kojaman claims that "(i)mprovisation is not considered to be a part of the Maqam tradition" (2001, 126).

9. Apparently named after the poet Mulla Jadir al-Zuhayri, who wrote in this dialect (Abu-Haidar 1988, 135).

10. This is also a characteristic feature of Persian and Mashreqi practices.

11. The anomolous 'Araibun Arab includes only qit'a and teslim.

12. See H. Rijab's discussion of these components in Elsner (1992, 162–83).

13. Cf., the identical meaning of the Persian term *daramad*.

14. B. Rijab (1985, 97) includes a single appearance of D♭; not found in other sources.

15. This also could be described as the naghmah Bastenegar.

16. According to Hamid al-Saadi (in Kojaman 2001, 171–76) and B. Rijab (1985, 18–21).

17. According to Scheherazade Hassan, the obscure maqam listings of Moussali (1996, 35)—Hayran, Shushtari, Akbari, Nahuft Arab, Zamzami, Ramal, Abu Ata, Qajar, Ma'rana—do not exist (personal communication, 2002).

18. Kojaman also credits Zaydan with the creation of maqam 'Araibun Arab (2001, 136).

19. Listed but not performed by Sha'oubi; also listed by Hamid al-Saadi. It likely denotes a tetrachord rather than a prescribed melody.

20. Warkov includes Bheirzawi (1987, 237).

21. Kojaman describes somewhat scandalous circumstances surrounding the creation of Tiflis, which may have contributed to its neglect in the repertoire (2001, 142).

22. Scheherazade Hassan's liner notes to the original LP edition of OCR 79 mention that some theorists also include maqam Awj.

23. The most common types descend 4 or 5-1 or are level (especially in the Hijaz family).

24. In terms of maqam scale, Beyat corresponds to Persian Shur, which is unquestionably the first dastgah of the radif.

25. There are clear hierarchical parallels between Iraqi maqam and the Persian radif: Baghdadi repertoire/radif; 7 basic maqams/7 dastgahs; derived maqam family/avaz or naghme; qit'a/gusheh.

An Anthology of Iraqi Maqam

1

The Rast Family

While Rast is arguably the most important maqam in terms of both theory and repertoire, this family is limited to Rast, Panjgah, and Sharqi Rast. The scale of Panjgah is that of Rast, while Sharqi Rast consists of Rast with ♭7; both are conventionally notated with F as tonic, in contrast to Rast (C tonic).

Rast

Rast is set to classical Arabic and uses the tahrir alfaz *Yar*; rhythmic accompaniment only appears for the two instrumental interludes of *dulab* Sharqi Rast (in the iqa's Wahda and Sengin Sama'i). There are two versions of maqam Rast—Rast Hindi and Rast Turki—the overall structures of which are virtually identical in terms of the content and ordering of qit'as, meyanas, interludes, and bridging passages. According to B. Rijab (1985, 43ff), the difference lies in the contents of their respective tahrirs and jalsas; Rast Turki seems to be the longer of the two maqams, partly because of extensions to these sections relative to those of Rast Hindi. Both tahrirs begin the same (zigzagging thirds reminiscent of the introduction to the Persian dastgah Mahur), but whereas Rast Hindi traces a 2-5-1 arch and proceeds directly to the definitive closing theme Nagriz, Rast Turki continues with some important contrasting modal qualities. The tetrachord below the tonic C is stressed (particularly A/6), and the D above is emphasized with a flattened alternation of G/5, which evokes Saba (on D). With one apparent exception, jalsas occur in the same places and even share similar materials.

Rast creates the effect of three meyanas with the inclusion of Hijaz Madani (which can be heard as the third meyana). In Yusuf Omar's performance Mathnawi is presaged by the second interlude, which juxtaposes Nahawand/1' and Rast 1. Full transcriptions of performances by Mohammed Qubanchi and Yusuf Omar (both Rast Hindi) are provided below. Note that Qubanchi adds to the standard form an extra section of Mansuri and a meyana-like qit'a (Beyat/5, with a hint of Saba) before the expected first meyana; Omar's rendering of Mansuri bears a striking similarity with the Persian gusheh Qarache (of dastgah Shur). Qubanchi's performance is particularly dense, featuring long sections and amazingly extended melismata. Warkov made an extensive etic analysis of Rast that corroborates the emic outline and provides many details of foreground and middle ground structure (1987, 248ff).

Other qit'a listed: Nari.

Mohammed Qubanchi performance:

Tahrir	Mans	Ibr?	J/HS	Mans	Beyat	Jls	Sh R	S Blb	Int	Khalili	Mathnawi	Teslim
1-6-7-1	5-8-5	2'-5	7-1	5-2'-5	8-4'-5	6-1	6-1	8-5'-1	5-7-1	4'-1-8	5- 8-3'-5	7-1
	Saba/5	Bey/5		Saba/5	Bey/5			Seg/3'			Hijaz/5	
							Wd 4/4		Wd 4/4			

Yusuf Omar performance:

Tahrir	Rast	Mans	Ibr	J/HS	S Blb	Jls	Sh R	Khalili	Int	H Md	Mathnawi	Teslim
1-6- 8-1	5-8-6-1	5- 8-5	7-5	7-1	8-5'-5	5-8-1	6-1	4'-5'-8	8-3'-1	8-8'-8	5-8-5'-5	6-8-1
		Saba/5			Seg/3'			Jhg/4'	Nah/8		Hijaz/5	
							Wd 4/4		SS 6/4			

Abbreviations: Bey=Beyat; H Md=Hijaz Madani; Ibr=Ibrahimi; Int=interlude; J/HS=Jalsa/Hijaz Shaytani; Jhg=Jahargah; Jls=Jalsa; Mans=Mansuri; Nah=Nahawand; S Blb=Segah Balban; Seg=Segah; Sh R=Sharqi Rast; SS=Sengin Sama'i; Wd=Wahda

Rast

Mohammed Qubanchi
(AAA-087)

1. Tahrir (0:18)

Yar   yar yar yar yar   yar   yar

yar   yar

yar   dao   yar   dao

a ja

2. Mansuri (1:43)

ah   dao   ya a yo su fal husn

ya yo su fal husn fe kas sab gad li ma   fa la u ra a'u ka ha wa'o

lil ar (thi)   fa la'u ra'uka ha w'a lil ar thi ta'a thi ma   a

a ya

3. (Ibrahimi?) (2:48)

di man   di man di man   di man ha ba ka fu

3   Jalsa/Hijaz Shaytani (3:05)

nun al husn a na la   bi man ha ba ka   fau nun al husn tak ri ma a la la la la

a la la la la

4. Mansuri (3:26)

ah

6

ya   be

5. Beyat (4:21)

ruh kaw ka ban   kaw ka ban   wa

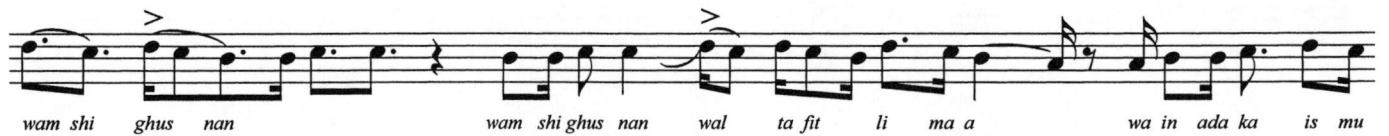

wam shi ghus nan   wam shi ghus nan wal ta fit li ma a   wa in ada ka is mu

ha   fa in a da ka is muha   a man   a man

a mana man   il it ya   3   3   3   3   3

a man

a man   a man   il it yam   a'u wad

yam   3   3   a 'u wad yam   a 'u wad a man

a man   a man   an a man   wa wa wa wa

a   ya   lil   ya

Jalsa (5:53)

do

Nagriz (6:08)

ya   dya

3   3   3

ra

Sharqi Rast interlude (6:29)

6. Segah Balban (no iqa') (7:06)

ya   da   ah

3

shah   dun   bi   tha gh ri ka

lam   lam   lam   lam tab rud bi   hi   ka bi dun

3

a man   bil shi   fi   ha   fi   ti   hi

3

(il   fa   dun)   a mana man   wa wa

3

a man a man   a   man   a   man   a   man   a   man

Dulab interlude (8:16)

man

7. Khalili (iqa' stops) (8:53)

na   za le   li man   tub di   tha lath   than   wa la   kin lam   ta na la ka ya dun

ya   *3*   *3*   *3*
                                                                                 ya

ya   liao ha   *3*   akh

ya   la   li   ya   la   li   ya   ya   ya

8. Mathnawi (9:55)

ya   da   yim   wa la kin   lam   ta nal   kaya   dun

waj' hun   waj' hun   a ghar rum   wa ji

dun   za na hu   gi ya   du   wa ga   ma tun   tukh ji   lul khi   ti   ya tag

wi   ma

9. Mathnawi (10:48)

                                                              3

ya   na zi lal   raml   min naj din   u hib   bu ku mu   buhib   bu ku mu   wa in ha

10. Mathnawi (11:15)

jer tum fo fi ma ha j ru kum fi ma ha ram

ta ha ram ta wa s li

11. Mathnawi (11:38)

ha ram ta wa s li ka ma hal lal ta saf ka da mi

tab bak tu sha ra ka tah lil lan watah ri ma

tab bak tu sha ra ka tah lil lan wa tah ri ma

Teslim (12:11)

o wa wa

Nagriz (12:31)

ya da ya da

Rast

Yusuf Omar
(Inedit 260063)

1. Tahrir (1:07)

Ya   *ya*

ya   *ya*

ya

2. Rast (2:44)

gha i ri 'al as sul wan   *gha i ri 'al as sul wan*   *'al as sul wan*   *i qa*

3. (3:35)

der wa si wa ya' fil 'ush sha qi gha   *dir gha i ri 'a la*

`a la   *(al)*   *'al as sul wan*   *i*

qa   *dir wa si wa*

(Nagriz)

fil ush sha   *qi gha*   *dir*

4. Rast (4:54)

li   *fil gha ram li*

fil gha ram

sa rir a (tun)   *sa rir a tun*   *wal lah*   *a' la mu bi*

sa ra   *'ir*   *li*   *fil gha ram*   *fil gha ram i sa ri ra tun*

wal lah a'   *la mu bil*   *sa rar*   *(ir)*

ah

5. Mansuri (6:33)

(wa) mu shab   *ba hun*   *bil ghusn wa mushab*   *ba hun*   *bil ghusn*   *bil*

bil

6. Mansuri (7:26)

(a)   *ah*

wa mush(abba) hun bil   *ghusn i qal bi*   *la*   *la ya zal*   *'a la i*   *hi ta' ir*   *ma na*

(Ibrahimi?)

ma

Jalsa/Hijaz Shaytani (7:59)

a man a na na   *na*   *na na na i*   *a na na na na*   *na*

7. Segah Balban (8:40)

la la la   *ya*   *da*

ah

a hul wal ha bib   wa in   na ha la ha la   wa tun sha qat ma ra

'ir   la ha la   wa tun   sha qat ma ra   ('ir)

Jalsa (9:30)

de la di   wa ya   dust   ma da da

(Nagriz)

ma ne ma ne   ma da da   ma na ma ne   e da

Sharqi Rast interlude in iqa' Wahda (9:52)

8. Khalili (10:38)

a   za li e   li man hul wul ha dith   wa in   na ha   ya

la a   lia ha

3

ya   la li ya   la li ya ya   ya

Interlude in iqa' Sengin Sama'i (11:26)

ya ba ya   ya nayim

9. Hijaz Madani (11:53)

a   *de man*

ya   *dost*   *na*   *da*   *na da da man*

Mathnawi (12:15)

a ya   *hul wul ha dith*   *i wa in na ha*   *la ha la wa tun*   *shaq qat ma ra*

10. Mathnawi (12:55)

'ir   *ash*   *ku*   *ash*   *ku ru*   *fi 'i la hu*   *ash*   *ku*   *ash*   *kuru*   *fi 'i la hu*

11. (13:41)

fa 'a jab   *bi sha*   *kin min hu sha*   *ker*   *ya lay lu dum*   *ya lay lu dum*

ya   *shaw qatul*   *ya lay la tul*   *ya*   *shaw*   *qa dum*   *in ni*

in   *ni*   *'a lal*   *ha*   *lay ni sa*   *bir*   *amanaman*

a   *na man*   *aman*   *a man*   *a man*   *wa*

Teslim (14:33)

in ni   *`a lal ha*   *lay ni sa bir*   *a*

a ra

Panjgah

Panjgah (or Banjgah) is set to classical poetry and is performed without rhythmic accompaniment. Sha'oubi uses the tahrir vocable *Ah*, while Hamid al-Saadi prescribes *Aman, bidad.* Iraqi Panjgah is characterized by an arching contour from 1 to (variously) 3, 4, 5, or 6, and returning to 1; it does not include the definitive #4 of the Turkish-Mashreqi Panjgah. The two contrasting qit'as of Sha'oubi's performance are of the generic tetrachord variety characteristic of his descriptions: both are in jins Hijaz on 5 (the second appearance of which functions as a meyana); D natural serves to steer the melody back to Panjgah (section 5 in the transcription). This modal contrast is parallel to the function of the qit'a I Mathnawi in maqam Rast. The jalsa and teslim consist of the same material, which descends to the qarar of the maqam on 5 before ending on 1.

Other qit'as listed: Mansuri, Mathnawi
Qit'a I appearance in maqam Sharqi Rast/Esfahan.

Sha'oubi Ibrahim performance:

Tahrir/bedwa	Panjgah (multiple repeats)	Hijaz	Panjgah	Jalsa	Meyana	Panjgah	Teslim
1-4-1	1-(4 or 5 or 6)-1	5-7-5	6-1	1-4-5-1	8-2'-5	5-1	1-4-5-1
		Hijaz/5			Hijaz/5		

Panjgah

Sha'oubi Ibrahim
(1982)

7. Meyana 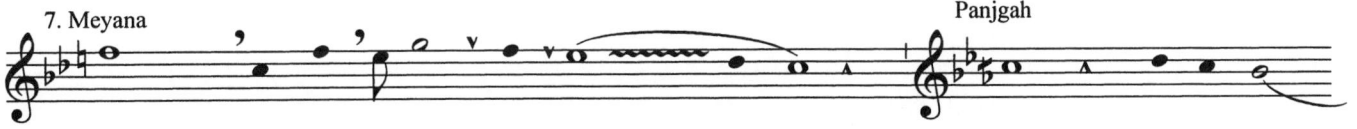 Panjgah

Teslim

Sharqi Rast/Esfahan

Sharqi Rast is set to iqa' Wahda with a *dulab*/refrain (entitled Sharqi Rast) that also occurs in maqams Rast and Sharqi Dogah. It features zheiri poetry, uses the tahrir alfaz *Yaba, ya, janam*, and has no meyana. Compared to maqams Rast and Panjgah, Sharqi Rast emphasizes the upper tetrachord and features a consistently flattened seventh degree. As presented by Sha'oubi, the qit'as Qatar and Mischin are not clearly separated and exposed but rather elide with the main mode of Sharqi Rast. Sharqi Rast bears some resemblance to the Persian avaz Afshari, particularly when it is juxtaposed with Qatar, which features a ♭6. Mischin also features a motive associated with Afshari (5-8-7-6-5), and cadences on A♭/3. The final qit'a, Panjgah, leads to the teslim, which uses the same material as maqam Panjgah's teslim.

Other qit'as listed: Mahmudi, Mukhalef, Taher.
Qit'a I appearance in maqams: Rashdi, Taher.

Sha'oubi Ibrahim performance:

Tahrir	Sharqi Rast	Sharqi Rast	Qatar	Sharqi Rast	Mischin	Sharqi Rast	Panjgah	Teslim
5-1	7-5/6-1	7-5	6-3	7-5	5-8-3	7-1	1-4 ; 5-1	1-4-5-1
			♭6					

Wahda 4/4

Sharqi Rast/Sharqi Esfahan

Sha'oubi Ibrahim
(1982)

Refrain

1. Tahrir

Yaba   ya ba   ya ba ya   ba ya   ba   ya   ya ba jan   am

2. Sharqi Rast

3. Sharqi Rast   4.   Qatar   5. Sharqi Rast   Mischin

6. Sharqi Rast   7. Panjgah

2

The Beyat Family

Members of the Beyat maqam family can differ with regards to transposition. Following Mashreqi conventions, the tonic pitch of Beyat is D. According to Sha'oubi Ibrahim (1982) other family members pitched at D are Bheirzawi, Mischin, and Mahmudi; G transpositions include Nari, Quriyat, and Sharqi Dogah; A transpositions include Ibrahimi, Juburi, and Mugabl (the latter two are sibling maqams that share a substantial amount of component material). Two or three types of melodic progressions are evident in the Beyat family. One type is a fairly direct descent from 5 (e.g., Mugabl, Sharqi Dogah) or 4 (Mahmudi and Juburi) to 1; Nari also features a 4-1 descent, but cadences on 2. Another type involves 1-4-1 progression (Mischin), which is prefixed in Bheirzawi as (1-3)-1-4-1, and extended in Ibrahimi as [3-7]-(1-3)-1-4-1. Mugabl also reflects this type of undulating return with its 5-1-4-1-3-1 progression. Quriyat features a curiously long and anomalous descent of 7-1. All Beyat family maqams (with the exception of maqam Beyat itself) are sung in the zheiri dialect, and are rhythmically accompanied (by iqa's Yugrug or Wahda), making it somewhat more difficult for quick identification; one must rely on their tahrir contents (i.e., alfaz, melodic contour, and thematic material) as guides. A glimpse of the basic themes of the obscure family members Quriyat and 'Araibun Arab (manifest as type I qit'as) is provided at the end of this chapter.

Beyat

Beyat is performed without rhythmic accompaniment, features classical poetry, and employs the tahrir alfaz *Aradeh, ah, ademan.* Iraqi Beyat shares key features with the Turkish-Mashreqi Beyati, including scale, melodic progression, motivic gestures, and idiomatic modulation; the opening gestures resemble the Persian gusheh Sayakhi of avaz-e Abu Ata. The main tahrir phrase consists of the archetypal descending arch, here outlining 4-1-4. A second theme for Beyat is an ascending arch emphasizing 6 and outlining 4-8-4; indeed, an essential feature of Beyat is that the ear is led to take 4 (which is usually reinforced by a drone) as the tonic of a Nahawand pentachord. Ambiguous allusion and full modulations to Jahargah (qit'a Lawouk I, the second meyana) and Ajam are idiomatic, as they are closely related in scale: Jahargah is the third octave species of Beyat, while performances of Ajam, which require a lowered 4 (E♭), generally avoid this note. The meyana straddles Rast and Beyat (at the apogee), a common, reciprocal ambiguity of both maqams that characterizes Turkish-Mashreqi practice as well. Saba is also an idiomatic modulation in Beyat and Turkish-Mashreqi cognates, although the Iraqi appearance in the sample here is very subtle, merely a brief taste (at 8:05 and 10:32 in Yusuf Omar's performance). Common motivic gestures include ascending 7-3 leaps before cadences, 6-5 continuous alternations (alluding to Ajam), and the most essential feature of Beyat: descents from 4-1.

There are some minor differences in the renditions of Beyat in the sources. Sha'oubi precedes Lawouk I with a phrase in Nawa (this is also apparent in Yusuf Omar's performance). Yusuf Omar adds another meyana (Scheherazade Hassan 1995a, 19) after Nahoft, which includes some material from the teslim and functions as a cadence that sets up the modulation to Ajam. Yusuf Omar's teslim is comparatively long, traversing the entire octave range twice. Qundarchi's concise version is apparently sung entirely in Persian (Moussali 1996, 45–45). It is largely unintelligible, however; such cavalier treatment of the text characterized many early reciters (Scheherazade Hassan 1995a, 16).

Other qit'as listed: Mthalatha, Qariabash, Saba.
Qit'a I appearance in maqams: Hijaz Diwan, Homayun, Khanabat, Nahawand, Nari, Nawa.

Rashid Qundarchi performance:

Tahrir	Beyat	Lwk	Beyat	Jalsa	Meyana	Nahoft	Lwk	Ajam	Beyat	Teslim
4-1-4	4-8-4	6-3	4-8-1	5-1	7-2'-5	7-3	7-4-3	6-8-4	4-1	5-1-7-7-1
					Rast/7			Ajam/6		

Yusuf Omar performance:

Tahrir	Beyat	Nawa?	Bey	Lwk	Bey	Jalsa	Mey 1	Nft	Lwk 2	Mey 2	Ajam	Beyat	Teslim
4-1-6-4	4-8-1-4	6-8-4	4-7-4	3-7-3	4-8-1	5-1	7-4'-4-7	8-3	7-2'-4	3-3'-3	6-3'-3-6	6-1	5-7-3'-1
		(♭8)			(♭4)		Rast/7		Nah/4			(♭4)	

Abbreviations: Bey=Beyat; Lwk=Lawouk; Mey=meyana; Nah=Nahawand; Nft=Nahoft

Beyat

Rashid Qundarchi
(Al Sur ALCD 183)

(??)

Jalsa (2:21)

a   da   wa

3   *3*

a   de   man

4. Meyana I (Rast) (2:52)

a di dei

3

(??)   *(sha   hi ma   ta   li dam shahi ma   ta   li   dam?)*

5. Nahoft (3:23)   Lawouk II   *3*

(??)   *ya   yei   yei   yei   yei yei   yei*

ya   yei   ya   yei

ya   *de*

Ajam (4:15)

ey

(??)

6. Beyat (4:42)

(??)   *(zama ne   za ma ne del ba ri lei li mo ha de the sah de qai di?)*

Teslim (4:56)

a   la   wa   *ya*   *de man*   *a   da*

de man   ya   *ana dei*

wa

Beyat

Yusuf Omar
(Inedit W.260063)

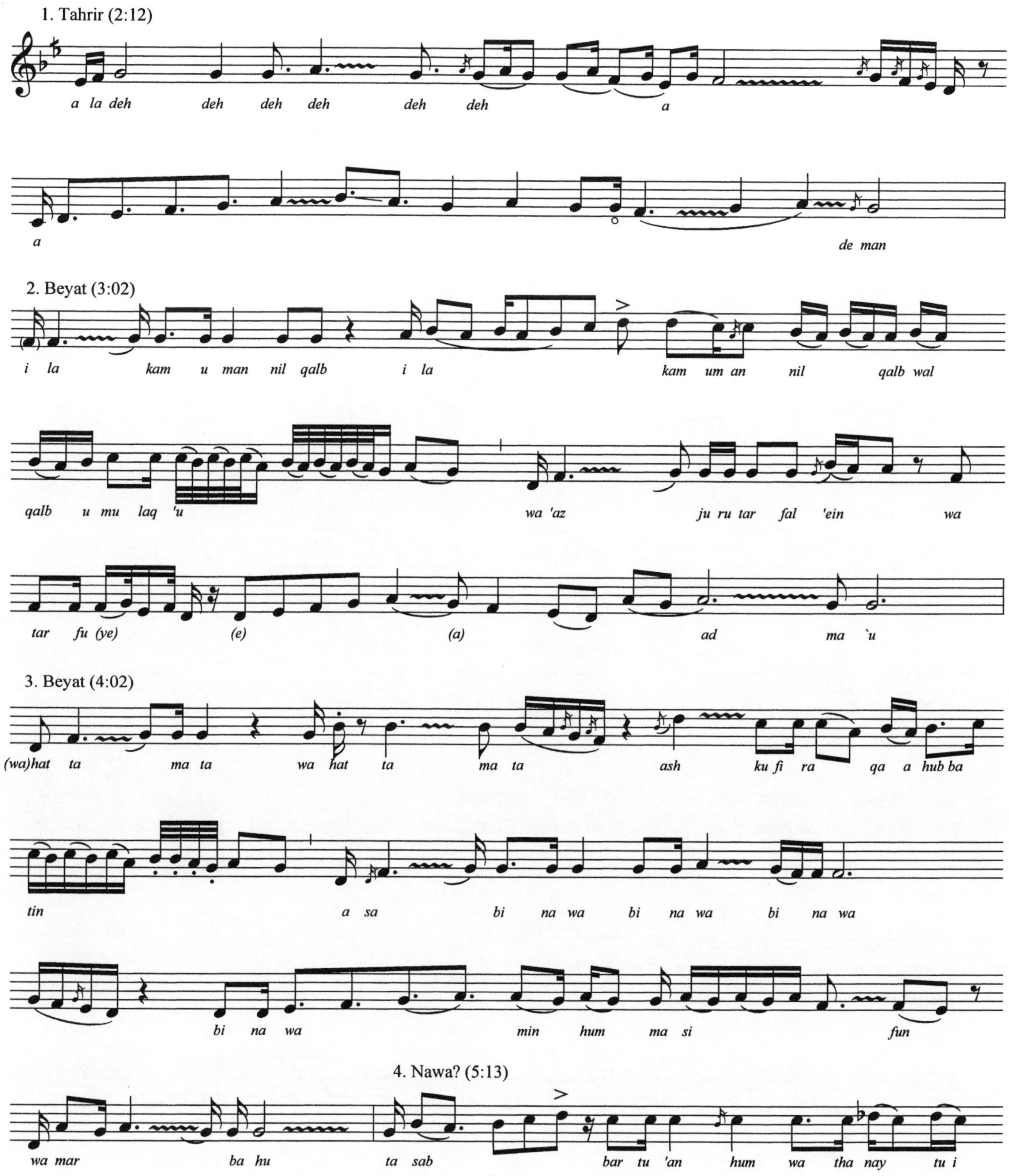

lay (hu mu)   wa lam   wa lam   wa lam   wa lam yab qa fi

(Beyat)

wa lam   yab qa fi   qow sit ta sa   as   bu (ni) ma

5. Beyat (6:25)

an   za`u   ta sab   bar tu an hum   wan tha nay tu(wan)   tha na

tu   wan tha nay   tu il ay (hu mu)   wa lam   yab qa fi

Lawouk (6:55)

a yeh   a   yeh   a yeh   a   yeh

yeh   a   yeh   a   yeh   a   yeh

6. Beyat (7:41)

a   gha rib   na shu mu san   gha rib   na sha

nu san fi   bu du ria kil la tin   wa lay   sa la ha il la min

(Saba)   Jalsa (8:11)

al khi dri mat la`u   a dya da   yar

ya   a   de man

Meyana (8:31)

(ali lay li lay luy lay) a lay sa la ha il la

fa lay sala ha il la minal minal minal minal a

al minal khi dri mat

Nahoft (9:01)

la bu a ya i a ya

ye ya a i a ya ya de

"Meyana II" (9:20)

man jan 3 nam jan nam

eh di le jan

7. Ajam (9:49)

u ra 'i nu ju mal leil (ar qibu) tay fa hum 6 fa kay

fa ya zu (ru) at tay fa man 3 fa kay fa ya zu ru(at) tay

6 6 Beyat (10:19)

fu man lay sa yah ja'u fa kay faya zu ru tay fu

Saba (10:32)

man   fa kay fa ya zu ru tay fu man

Teslim (10:36)

a dya da ya a ma

a   de man   i le ja

ma de man jan an jan

am   e di la de eh weh

weh weh weh wa wa a de man

Bheirzawi

Bheirzawi is set to zheiri poetry in the iqa' Yugrug and employs the tahrir alfaz *Ah, kheyyi, la la le*; it has no meyana. It features an undulating contour whereby qit'as begin on 7, 5, or 4 and descend to 1 (many phrases bear a resemblance to Persian Shur, particularly the characteristic motive 7-3-1). There are several qit'as from the Beyat family (Qariabash and Quriyat appear as subtle variants of each other in Sha'oubi's performance) and a diversion to Jahargah in its final portion. After repeating the refrain, Sha'oubi's joze introduces Sayha Mahmudi (at section 7) with a motive that creates the effect of shifting the tonal center to 4. The qit'a in jins Rast (alternately known as Mischin) is not sung but rather performed on the joze. The first phrase of the tahrir also functions as the teslim.

Other qit'as listed: Ibrahimi, Khanabat, Mthalatha, 'Omar Gala.
Qit'a I appearance in maqams: 'Araibun Arab, Ibrahimi, Mugabl, Rashdi.

Sha'oubi Ibrahim performance:

Tahrir	Bhz	Mgb	Bhz	Qbsh	Juburi	Qryt	S Mah	Aboush	Qatar	Jhg	Rast	Bhz	Teslim
1-4-1	1-7-1	5-1	7-3-1	7-5-1	4-1	7-5-1	4	4-1	4-5-3	3-5-1	7-4-1	6-1	7-4-1
						♮6			♭5		Rast/7		

Yugrug 12/4

Abbreviations: Bhz=Bheirzawi; Jhg=Jahargah; Mgb=Mugabl; Qbsh=Qariabash; Qryt=Quriyat; S Mah=Sayha Mahmudi

Bheirzawi

Sha'oubi Ibrahim
(1982)

Refrain ... "turnaround" or tacit

1. Tahrir

Ah   *khe yi*   *khe yi*   *khe yi*

ya   *la le*   *la le*   *la*   *kheyi*

2. Bheirzawi

3. Mugabl   **4. Bheirzawi**   Qariabash

5. Juburi   **6. Quriyat**

7. joze intro   Sayha Mahmudi/Aboush

Ah

8. Qatar

9. Jahargah

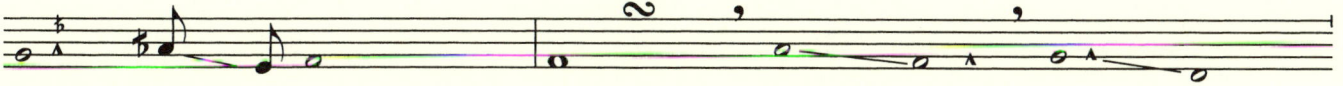

jins Rast/Mischin (joze solo)

Bheirzawi

a   ma'   wed

ah

Teslim

khe   yi

Ibrahimi

Ibrahimi features zheiri poetry accompanied throughout by iqa' Yugrug; its tahrir alfaz are *Ah, kheyi*. Ibrahimi is remarkable for its unprecedentedly large collection of qit'as, which include representatives of all basic maqams with the exception of Husseini and Nawa. In this respect Ibrahimi corresponds to the Persian dastgahs of Mahur and Rast Panjgah, functioning as a "sampler" of the entire repertoire. 'Ataba Zanburi is among the qit'as of Ibrahimi, imported from the tradition of Iraqi folk recitation (cf., Rukbani in maqam Hakimi and Zaza in maqam Orfa).

The presentation of Ibrahimi in Sha'oubi is particularly abbreviated, with extremely brief allusions to most qit'as (Mansuri is reduced to a miniscule ♭4 upper-neighbor gesture), which follow rather continuously with occasional iterations of the refrain or fragments of it. Though customarily set at G, Sha'oubi presents the maqam with an A tonic. Due to the unwieldy number of qit'as, I will forgo the usual schematic diagram of the maqam and merely list the qit'as, whose profiles and modality are accessible through the transcription.

Qit'as in Sha'oubi Ibrahim performance: Tahrir (jins Segah, jins Rast), Ibrahimi, Nari, Sayha, Sunbule, 'Araibun Ajam, Beyat, Qarar, Taher, 'Omar Gala, Quriyat, Sayha, Mansuri, Qariabash, Aboush, Sayha Mahmudi, Qatar, Mugabl, Bheirzawi, Juburi, Sayha, 'Ataba Zanburi, Mischin/Rast, refrain modulation to Jahargah, 'Alizabar/'Ardhibar, Teslim.

Other qit'as listed: Humaydiyya, Khanabat, Mthalatha, Qazaz.
Qit'a I appearances in maqams: Bheirzawi, Hijaz Diwan, Husseini, Rast.

Ibrahimi

Sha'oubi Ibrahim
(1982)

Refrain

"turnaround" or tacit

1. Tahrir/jins Segah

Ah   kheyi

2. Ibrahimi

(jins Rast)

3. Nari

4. Sayha   Ibrahimi

Ah kheyi   *Ya ba*

Sunbule   5. 'Araibun Ajam   Beyat

Mena lale   *Ah*   *lil*

Qarar   Taher   6. 'Omar Gala   Quriyat

Ya lil ya   lil   *alulelule   ayaya*

Sayha   Mansuri   Qariabash   Aboush   7. Sayha Mahmudi

La galby   *Babeh*   *Ah*   *Ah*

Qatar   Mugabl   Bheirzawi   Juburi

Mena wil

8. Sayha   'Ataba Zanburi

Wila 'eyuni yamdel

Mischin/Rast   (joze)

Ya ba   *Ya ba.*

(refrain in Jahargah)

9. 'Ardhibar/'Alizabar

Diya ya

Teslim

Wai wai   *Mena 'alit . . .*   *ya*

Ah   *kheyi*

Juburi

Juburi is set to zheiri poetry, accompanied by iqa' Yugrug and employs the tahrir alfaz *La, la waleh, galby*. The melodic progression of Juburi is a concise distillation of the archetypal Beyat 4-1 descent; qita I appearances often feature alternate open and closed cadences (i.e., on 7 and 1), evident in section 10 of Sha'oubi's performance.

Other qit'as listed: Humaydiyya, Mthalatha, Sunbule.
Qit'a I appearance in maqams: Arwah, Bheirzawi, Husseini, Ibrahimi, Mahmudi, Mugabl, Nawa, Taher, Orfa.

Sha'oubi Ibrahim performance:

Tahrir	Juburi	Qariabash	Mugabl	Qatar	jins Beyat	Quriyat	Juburi	Omar Gala	Juburi	Teslim
4-1	4-1	6-1	5-1-4-1-3-1	4-3	6-1	5-7-1	4-1	4-1	4-1	4-2-4-1
				♭5		♮6				

Yugrug 12/4

Juburi

Sha'oubi Ibrahim
(1982)

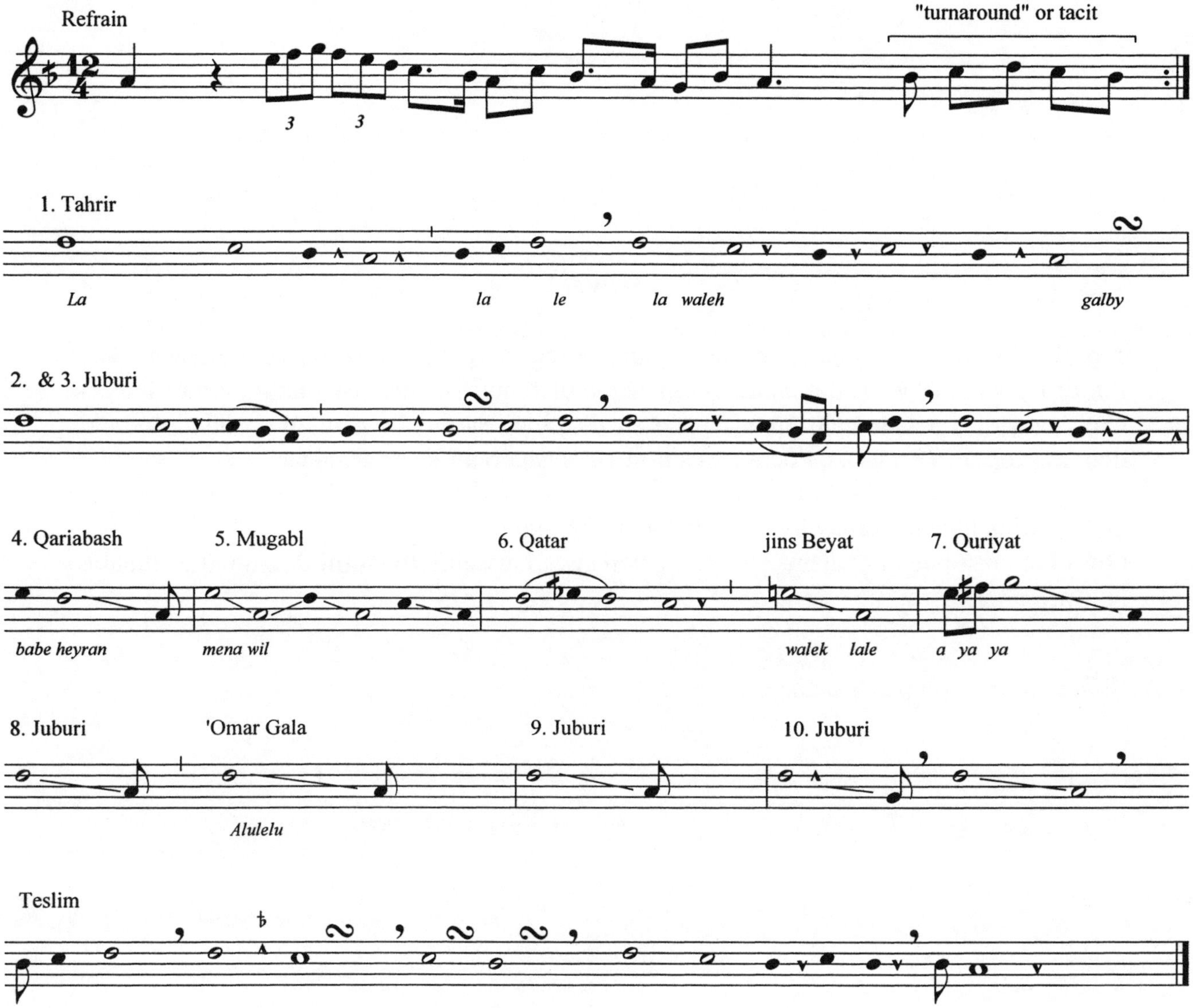

Mahmudi

Mahmudi features zheiri poetry, iqa' Yugrug and the tahrir alfaz *La waleh, ya 'eyuni.*
Mahmudi is performed in the upper register to the end of qit'a Qariabash, at which point
its successive descents create a tumbling contour. The integral Beyat motive 1-7-3-1 concludes the tahrir and teslim.

Other qit'as listed: Aboush, 'Alizabar.
Qit'a I appearances in maqams: 'Araibun Arab, Bheirzawi, Hadidi, Ibrahimi, Mukhalef,
Nawa, Saba, Sharqi Rast, Taher.

Sha'oubi Ibrahim performance:

Tah	Mah	Say	Jub	Say	Seg	Mgb	Mth	Qbsh	Say	O Gl	Qryt	Say	desc	Jhg	Aid	Jhg	Tes
4-2-4	4-1	4-2-4	4-1	4-2-4	4-2	5-1	5-1	4-7-1	4-2-4	4-1	5-1	4-2-4	1-1	3-1	1-3	3	5-1
					Seg/2			♮6									

Yugrug 12/4

Abbreviations: Aid=Aidin; desc=descent; Jhg=Jahargah; Jub=Juburi; Mah=Mahmudi;
Mth=Mthalatha; Mgb=Mugabl; O Gl='Omar Gala; Qryt=Quriyat; Qbsh=Qariabash;
Say=Sayha; Seg=Segah; Tah=Tahrir; Tes=Teslim

Mahmudi

Sha'oubi Ibrahim
(1982)

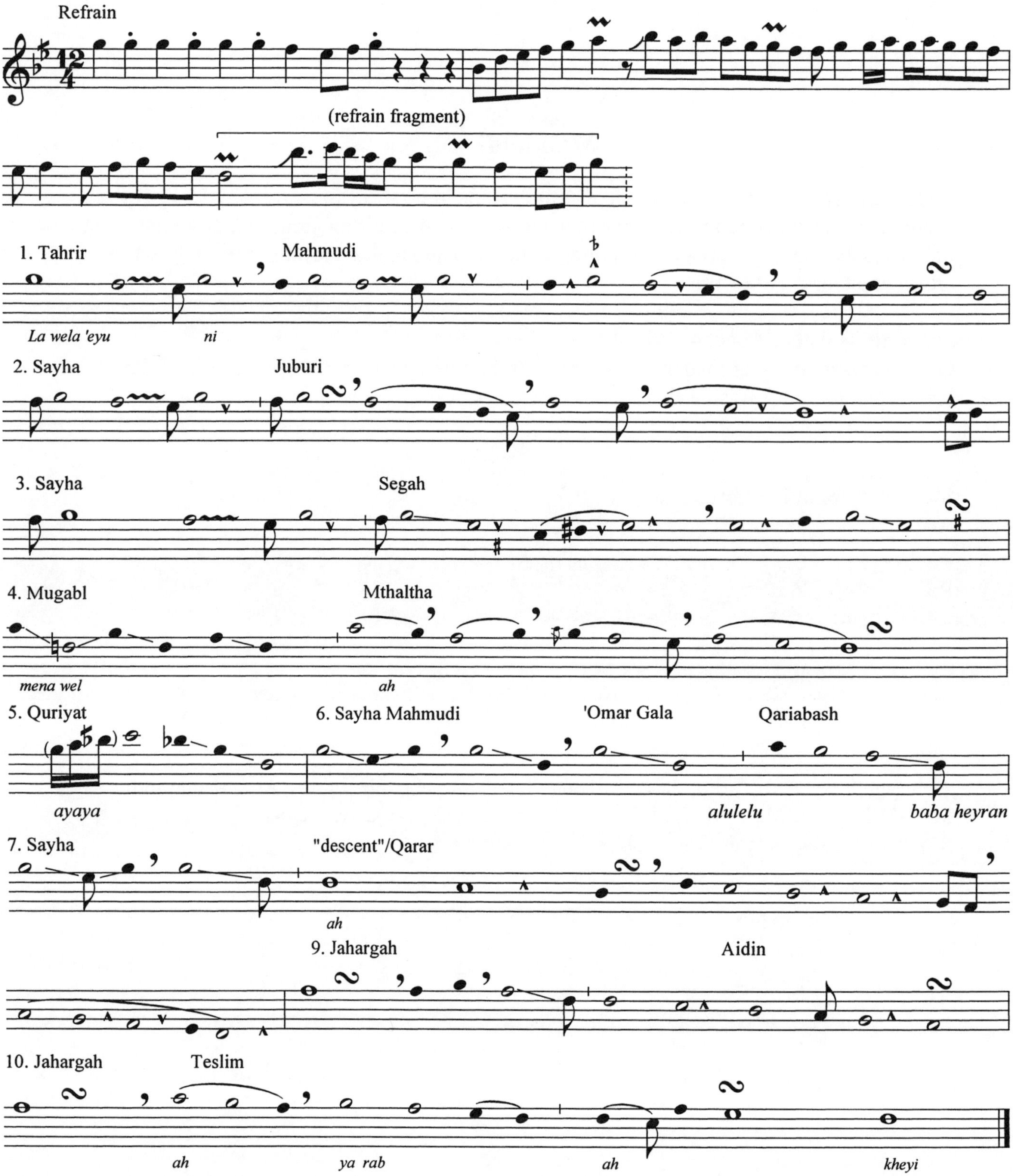

Mischin

Mischin is set to zheiri poetry and accompanied by iqa' Wahda. Sha'oubi employs the tahrir alfaz *La bila galbi,* Hamid al-Saadi, *Manala, walla, galbi.* Sha'oubi's intonation in the performance is at odds with his prescriptions: Sayha Mahmudi is sung with a ♭5, and qit'a Ajam sounds closer to Rast. The maqam remains in the upper register until the teslim, which descends to the lower octave tonic. The vocable used for the teslim (*mischin*) is the name of the maqam itself, reminiscent of the musical punning that characterizes the Turkish compositional genre *kari natik.*

Other qit'as listed: Aidin, Mthalatha, Mugabl
Qit'a I appearances in maqams: Bheirzawi, Ibrahimi, Mugabl, Sharqi Rast.

Sha'oubi Ibrahim performance:

Tahrir	Mischin	Sayha Mahmudi	jins Ajam	Ajam	Juburi	Mischin	Teslim
1-4-1	7-4-1	4-3	4-3	4-3	4-1	1-4-2	1-1

Wahda 4/4

Mischin

Sha'oubi Ibrahim
(1982)

Mugabl

Mugabl features zheiri poetry, the tahrir alfaz *Mena wel, awel*, and is accompanied by iqa' Yugrug. There is no teslim: the maqam ends with a repetition of Mugabl itself. The qit'as Qatar and 'Araibun Ajam listed in Sha'oubi are extremely abbreviated.

Other qit'as listed: Aboush, Madmi, Mischin, Mthalatha, 'Omar Gala, Qariabash.
Qit'a I appearances in maqams: Bheirzawi, Hadidi, Hakimi, Hijaz Kar, Ibrahimi, Juburi, Mahmudi, Mischin, Segah.

Sha'oubi Ibrahim performance:

Tahrir	Mugabl	Juburi	Quriyat	Qatar	Bheirzawi	'Araibun Ajam	Mugabl
5-1-4-1-3-1	5-1-4-1-3-1	4-1	5-7-1	4-5-3	1-7̱-3-1	4	5-1-4-1-3-1
			(♮6)	♭5		Hijaz/1	

Yugrug 12/4

Mugabl

Sha'oubi Ibrahim
(1982)

Refrain

"turnaround" or tacit

1. Tahrir

Mena wel

2. Mugabl

3. Juburi

4. Quriyat

5. Qatar

6. Bheirzawi

a ya yai

7. 'Araibun Ajam

8. Mugabl

mena wel

Nari

Nari is set to zheiri poetry and accompanied by iqa' Yugrug (Kojaman cites iqa' Ay Nawasi [2001, 155]). While there are no tahrir alfaz identified in the text, Sha'oubi sings the syllables *Eliye*; Hamid al-Saadi prescribes *Billah* or *Billah ya rab*. While Sha'oubi describes the transposition of the Beyat scale as D in Nari (1982, 94), his performance and transcription of the pesta is in G. Nari cadences on 2, which hints at a "foil" relationship with Segah. The opening gesture of its theme is reminiscent of maqam Mahmudi. The scale, melodic contour, and cadential feature of Nari has affinities with the Persian avaz Abu Ata. Sha'oubi's performance features the substantial strophic repetition of Nari; the alfaz of his rendition of the teslim include the name of the maqam itself (cf., maqam Mischin).

Other qit'as listed: Quriyat, Sufyan.
Qit'a I appearances in maqams: Hleilawi, Ibrahimi, Rashdi, Rast.

Sha'oubi Ibrahim performance:

Tahrir	Nari	Mukhalef	Nari	Mthalatha	Nari	Nari	Teslim
4-7-2	4-7-2	4-2	4-7-2	5-1	4-7-2	4-7-2	4-1
		Mukhalef/2					

Yugrug 12/4

Nari

Sha'oubi Ibrahim
(1982)

Sharqi Dogah

While Sha'oubi affiliates Sharqi Dogah with the Beyat family, the polarization of 5 that characterizes the maqam bears more affinity with the Husseini family; this maqam does, however, end with a clear Beyat 4-1 progression. It is accompanied throughout by the 'iqa Wahda, and features a transposed version of the melody Sharqi Rast (from maqams Sharqi Rast and Rast) as its refrain. It is set to zheiri poetry; Sha'oubi employs the tahrir alfaz *La bile, galbak wa galbi* (cf., maqam Hadidi), Hamid al-Saadi, *La walla galbi, labela ya ghanem.* The qit'as Orfa, Arwah, and 'Ushaish (which has a cadential function in the context of maqams Sharqi Dogah and Husseini) are all close variants related to Husseini and here represent subtle melodic, rather than modal, changes. The character of Sharqi Dogah itself is melismatic.

Other qit'a listed: Zaza.

Sha'oubi Ibrahim performance:

Tahrir	Sharqi Dogah	Orfa	Arwah	'Ushaish	Sharqi Dogah	Sharqi Dogah	Teslim
5-7-1	5-7-1	5-7-4	5-7-5	5-1	5-6-1	5-7-1	1-3-<u>7</u>-1

Wahda 4/4

Sharqi Dogah

Sha'oubi Ibrahim
(1982)

Refrain

1. Tahrir

La bile   la bi le   la bi le   la   bile la   bile galbek

wa gal bi ya   ba ya   ba ya   ya gha nim

2. Sharqi Dogah

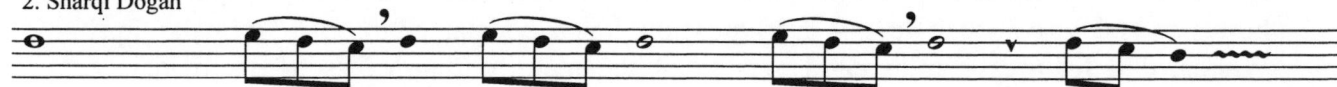

ya   ya 'e yu   ni

3. Sharqi Dogah

ya ba ya ba ya

4. Orfa

ya   ya   gha   nim

5. Arwah   **'Ushaish**

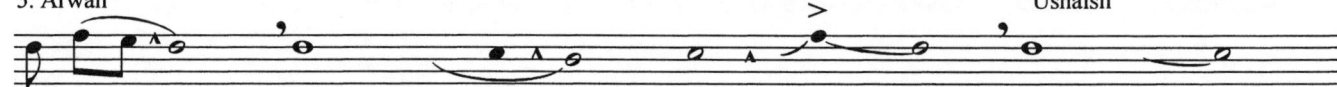

wa yai

6. Sharqi Dogah

akh akha

7. Sharqi Dogah   **Teslim**

ya   ya 'e yu   ni

Themes of Other Beyat Maqams

Sha'oubi Ibrahim
(1982)

Quriyat as qit'a I

(in maqam Bheirzawi)

(in Mugabl)

(in Juburi)

'Araibun Arab

(in maqam 'Araibun)

3

The Husseini Family

With the ambiguous exception of maqam Husseini itself, members of the Husseini family all polarize 5 and are thereby clearly aligned with Turkish-Mashreqi versions of Husseini. Sha'oubi (1982) uses D for the tonic pitch of family members Arwah and Dasht; Orfa is in G. Orfa and Arwah maintain the rather inconsistent and theoretical ♭6 of Husseini, while Dasht uses ♭6. Further melodic distinctions involve characteristic motives, cadence tones (Orfa features a unique 3-4 cadence), and progressions descending to 1 (except for Orfa, which eventually terminates on 5). While Sha'oubi places maqam Sharqi Dogah in the Beyat family, it has some affinities of the Husseini family, with its emphasis on 5.

Husseini

Maqam Husseini is set to classical Arabic poetry and is performed without rhythmic accompaniment. Sha'oubi employs the alfaz *Ah;* Yusuf Omar *Ah yademan;* Hamid al-Saadi prefixes the later with *Feryademan, yar yademan.* B. Rijab (1985, 96) describes three short versions of the modally ambiguous tahrir, which are followed by a standard closing phrase (Yusuf Omar uses the first of these). While there are occasional suggestions of an implied tonic of D (and therefore a parallel with Turkish-Mashreqi Husseini), I follow Iraqi theoretical conceptions by maintaining A as the tonic. Husseini is a strophic maqam with a compound structure: a polarity of short, alternating phrases of what Sha'oubi (1982, 34–35) describes as Rast on G to accompany the first half of the poetic couplet (marked "A" in the transcription) and Beyat on A with the second (marked "B"). Yusuf Omar's rendering of the "A" phrase evokes Jahargah on C, a descending corresponding to what B. Rijab and Sha'oubi describe as qit'a Khalwati. These shifting centers are underscored by moving drones in Yusuf Omar's performance. The meyanas of Husseini are quite brief, variants of the same phrase; Yusuf Omar omits the first appearance of the short qit'a Buselik and the following jalsa. B. Rijab (1985, 98) notes three short meyana variants that descend to from 3' to either 5 or 4. In the jalsa and teslim the maqam descends (and ends) on A below middle C; the Iraqi name of this pitch is Husseini 'Usheiran, hence the full name of the maqam.

With respect to key signatures B. Rijab (1985, 93) indicates only B♭, while Sha'oubi (1982, 34) includes B♭ and E♭. B. Rijab describes 6 in ascending (kar diyes) and descending (natural) forms—a characteristic feature of Turkish and Mashreqi cognates—but does not use the raised form in his transcription of the maqam. In Sha'oubi the quality of the upper E appears regularly as ♭3 of Rast phrases. B. Rijab and Yusuf Omar use E♮ exclusively, in the context of ♮3 of Jahargah phrases (i.e., Khalwati) and ♮5 of Beyat phrases (including meyanas). Amiri's transcription of Qubanchi's performance follows Sha'oubi's usage, but also occasionally includes an anomalous E♭ functioning as ♭5 of Beyat phrases.

Other qit'as listed: Arwah, Ibrahimi, Mthalatha, Saba.
Qit'a I appearances in maqams: Arwah, Dasht, Hijaz Diwan, Lami, Mansuri, Orfa, Taher.

Yusuf Omar performance:

Tahrir	Husseini strophe		Mey 1	Hus	Hus	Mey 2	Hus	Hus	Jub?	Hus	Bus	Tes
6-3-3-1	3-7	3-6-1	6-1	3-6-1	3-6-1	6-1	3-6-1	3-6-1	4-1	3-6-1	2-4	6-1
	Jhg/3	Bey/1									(♭2)	

Abbreviations: Bey=Beyat; Bus=Buselik; Hus=Husseini strophe; Jhg=Jahargah; Jub=Juburi; Mey=Meyana; Tes=Teslim

Husseini

Yusuf Omar
(Ocora C.580066)

1. Tahrir (1:53)

Ah ... *ya* ... *deman ya* ... *ah* ... *de man* ... *eh* ... *ah*

2. Husseini (3:28)   ("A" phrase, cf., Khalwati)

("B" phrase)

3. Husseini (4:59)

Meyana (5:24)

ah

Husseini (5:41)

4. Husseini (7:09)

5. Husseini (8:27)

6. Meyana (9:34)

ya   dust   ah   *3*

Husseini

7. Husseini (11:04)   Juburi?

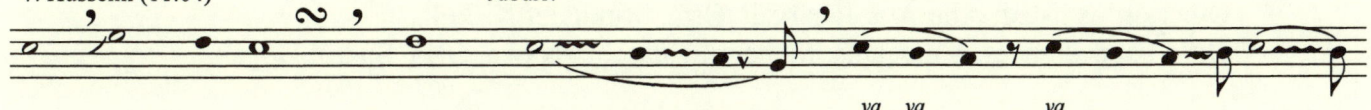

ya   ya   ya

(Husseini)

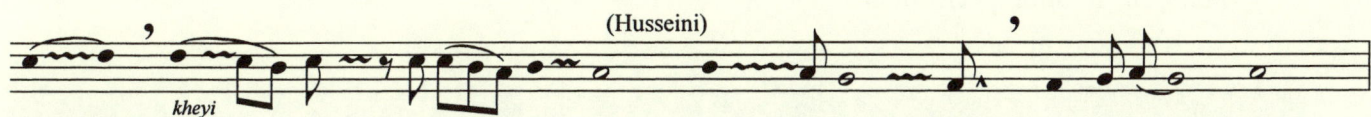

kheyi

8. Husseini (12:38)

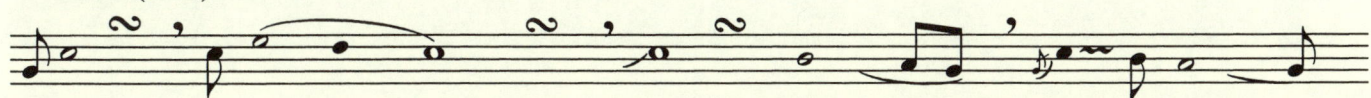

(13:30) Buselik   Teslim

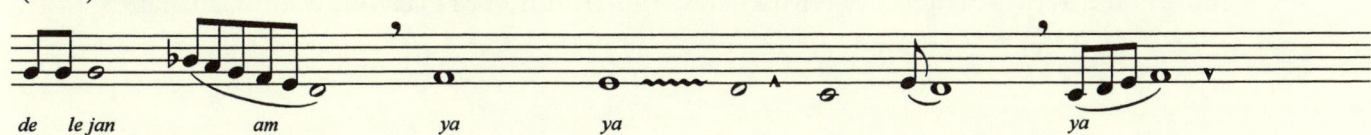

de   le jan   am   ya   ya   ya

ya   ya

Arwah

Arwah is performed with classical Arabic poetry, employs the tahrir alfaz *Mena billah, ya haili*, and is accompanied by iqa' Wahda (Sha'oubi uses the refrain from maqam Orfa). It displays some affinities of the Turkish-Mashreqi Husseini and Persian Dashti, featuring the characteristic polarization of 5, a 5-4-3 progression that eventually cadences on 1, and a distinctive 5-4-7-5 motive. The quality of 6, which is generally avoided or merely ornamental in Arwah itself, oscillates between B♭ and B♮ in Sha'oubi's performance. The qit'a 'Ushaish functions here as both an appendage to the tahrir and as the teslim; all the qit'as appear as juxtaposed pairs in Sha'oubi's presentation. Mukhalef is given an interesting transposition with A as its tonic (as opposed to its idiomatic kar bimol root position).

Other qit'as listed: Abu Ata, Jahargah, Orfa, Mukhalef Kirkuk.
Qit'a I appearances in maqams: Mansuri, Husseini, Nawa, Orfa, Sharqi Dogah.

Sha'oubi Ibrahim performance:

Tah	Arw	Ush	Mkh	Kyn	Hus	Jub	Arw	Ush	Dasht	HGhr	Arw	Taher	Tes/Ush
7-3-5	7-3-5	5-1	8-5	8-5	8-4	8-5	7-3-5	5-1	6-7-1	4-5-1	7-3-5	3	5-1
			♭7	Bey/5					(♮5)	Hjz/1			

Wahda 4/4

Abbreviations: Arw=Arwah; Bey=Beyat; HGhr=Hijaz Gharib; Hjz=Hijaz; Hus=Husseini; Jub=Juburi; Kyn=Kuyani; Mkh=Mukhalef; Tah=Tahrir; Tes=Teslim; Ush='Ushaish

Arwah

Sha'oubi Ibrahim
(1982)

Refrain

1. Tahrir   Arwah

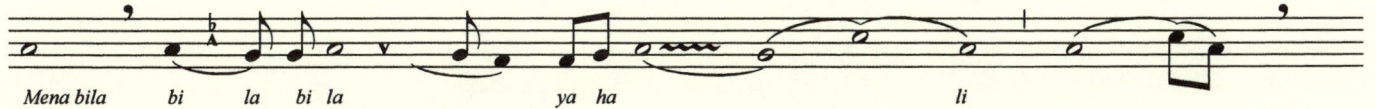

Mena bila   bi   la   bi la   ya ha   li

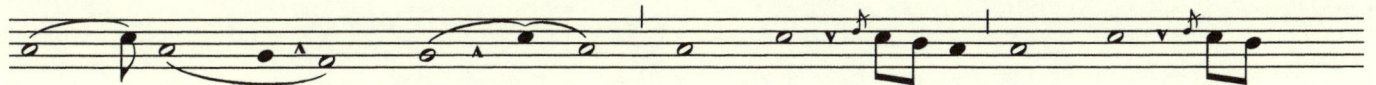

'Ushaish

wayei   akha

2. Mukhalef

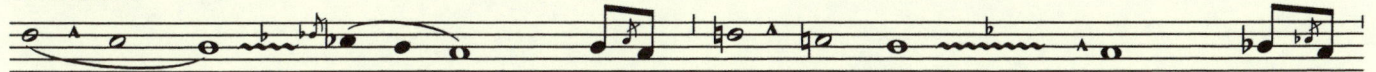

Kuyani   3. Husseini

ya yab   ischem ya yab

Juburi   4. Arwah

'Ushaish   5. Dasht

wayei   *akha*

                                                          6. Hijaz Gharib

7. Arwah

8. Taher   Teslim/'Ushaish

                    wayei   *akha*

Dasht

The three pronouns Dasht, Dashti, and Dasht 'Arab occur inconsistently in the literature in reference to two different maqams of the Iraqi repertoire; I arbitrarily follow Sha'oubi's designation of Dasht for the more common of the two. Dasht is performed without rhythmic accompaniment and set to classical Arabic poetry. Sha'oubi employs the tahrir alfaz *Awa, ah*; Hamid al-Saadi *Away yar, ah aman, janem*. Clearly related to the Persian avaz Dashti, it was imported and adapted by Ahmad Zaydan. Sha'oubi's tahrir in Dasht is limited to a short 3-2-1 descent, while the main modality reflects definitive features of the Persian source, particularly in sections 3 and 5 of Sha'oubi, the latter of which includes the idiomatic ♮/♭ alteration of 5. The motive 5-7-6-5 is characteristic of the maqam; some phrases descend to 1, others cadence on 5 (approached from either above or below). The short meyana (section 6 in Sha'oubi) corresponds to the Persian gusheh Oj of avaz-e Dashti. Qit'as Lami and Hijaz Gharib (a strikingly contrasting modulation) are interesting and exclusively Iraqi, without parallels in the Persian model.

Other qit'as listed: Abu Ata, Arwah, Hijaz Diwan, Orfa.
Qit'a I appearance in maqams: Arwah, Hijaz Diwan, Huizawi, Lami, Orfa.

Sha'oubi Ibrahim performance:

Tahrir	Dasht	Sayha	Lami	Hijaz Gharib	Husseini	Teslim
3-1	5-7-5; 5-7-1	8-5	5-2	4-1	5-8-5	5-7-1
		Beyat/5	♮2	Hijaz/1	Husseini/5	

Dasht

Sha'oubi Ibrahim
(1982)

1. Tahrir

Dasht

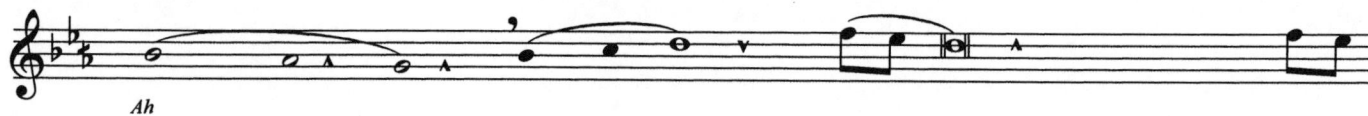

Ah

2. Dasht

3. Dasht

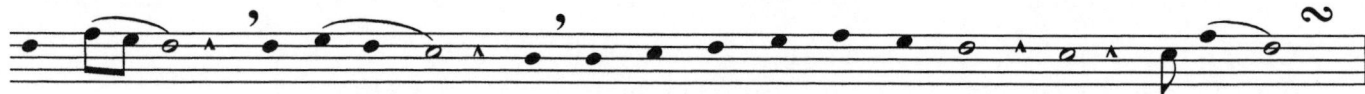

4. Dasht

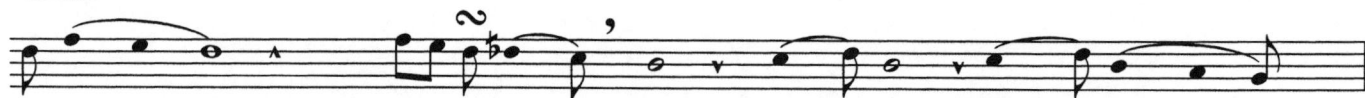

5. Dasht

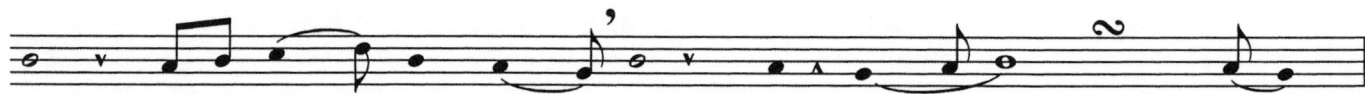

6. Sayha/Meyana

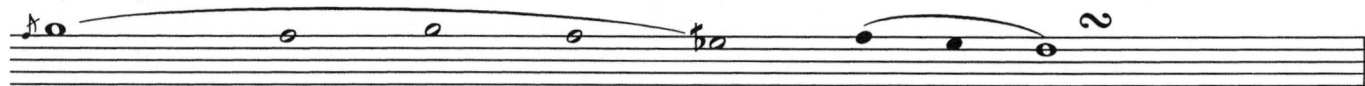

Ah

7. Lami

Hijaz Gharib   **8. Husseini**

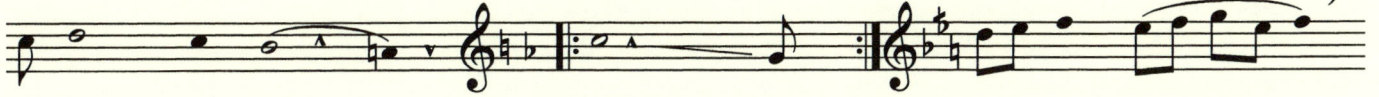

Teslim

Orfa

Orfa is set to the iqa' Wahda Tawila with classical Arabic poetry; there is no meyana. Sha'oubi uses the tahrir alfaz *Ah*; Hamid al-Saadi *Aman oghlem*. As performed by Sha'oubi, the main modality of Orfa is characterized by various progressions of 5-7-5 or 5-7-4; there are idiomatic half-cadences on 4 (especially 3-4), and the maqam does not descend to 1 until the teslim. A characteristic ornamental feature of Orfa is a minor third leaping gesture, indicated in the transcription by the upper-neighbor note symbol with a grace note. The qit'a Zaza, which appears to be a variant of Orfa itself, is derived from Iraqi folk music.

Other qit'as listed: Hijaz Diwan, Lami, Lawouk, Mthalatha, Mukhalef.
Qit'a I appearance in maqams: Arwah, Sharqi Dogah.

Sha'oubi Ibrahim performance:

Tahrir	Orfa	Orfa	Arwah	'Ushaish	Husseini	Orfa	Dasht	Juburi	Zaza	Orfa	Teslim
5	5-7-4	5-7-5	5-3-7-5	4-1	7-4; 8-5	5-3	7-5-1	8-5	8-5	5-7-1	3-1
					Husseini/ 5		Bey/1 (♭5)	Bey/1			
Wahda Tawila 2/4											

Abbreviations: Bey=Beyat

Orfa

Sha'oubi Ibrahim
(1982)

Refrain

1. Tahrir

Ah   *ah*

2. Orfa

3. Orfa

4. Orfa

(Arwah)   'Ushaish   **5. Husseini**   Orfa

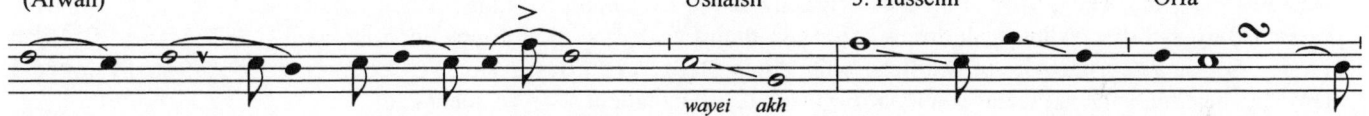

wayei   akh

Dasht

6. Juburi   **7. Zaza**

8. Orfa   Teslim

ah

4

The Hijaz Family

Sha'oubi performs Hijaz family maqams with a tonic of G, with the exception of Hijaz Diwan (on D) and Hijaz Kar (on C). Al-Basri (1996) assigns Huizawi, Madmi, and 'Araibun Ajam tonics of D. After scale, the most important feature of "international Hijaz" is the polarization of 4, a property found in four of seven family members in Sha'oubi. Madmi approaches 4 from above, intones it extensively before a quick final descent to 1. Huizawi and 'Araibun Ajam both polarize and cadence on 4 (Huizawi approaches it directly from above, while 'Araibun Ajam works up from below [7,1, or 2]). Clearly differentiated from this group are Homayun, which polarizes 1 (with a secondary emphasis on 2), and Hijaz Kar, which features a different upper tetrachord from other family members, as well as a distinct 8-1 descending contour. Sha'oubi's performance of Qatar includes only ornamental traces of the essential augmented second interval of Hijaz.

Hijaz Diwan

Hijaz Diwan is set to classical Arabic poetry and is accompanied by iqa' Wahda, which begins before the meyana. Sha'oubi employs the tahrir alfaz *Faryade man*; Hamid al-Saadi *Yademan deyay*. A profound and plaintive maqam, Hijaz Diwan bears a striking resemblence to the Persian gusheh Bidad (and the latter's group of variants or satellite gushehs). The name Diwan refers to 5 (i.e., the scale degree normally called Husseini) in the context of this maqam (Scheherazade Hassan 1995a, 21). The quality of 6 varies between flat and kar bimol; B. Rijab (1985, 73) accounts for this by referring to ascending and descending scale forms. Although things are not so tidy in practice, Sha'oubi (1982, 54) and B. Rijab (1985, 73) use a key signature of two flats, while Amiri (1990, 116) uses E♭ and B♭. Curiously, none indicate the raised 3 (F♯), the most fundamental scalar feature of the maqam, but include it as an accidental.

The same melody of the tahrir is repeated for several *beyts* (couplets) of poetry. Formal sections and components feature the compounding of smaller units. Yusuf Omar's performance of Husseini includes the short meyana phrase from that maqam in section four (at 5:27). The jalsa, signalled by a poignant A♭, is relatively extended, consisting of three or four phrases including the qit'a Nagriz. A prescribed *dulab* in iqa' Wahda precedes the meyana (qit'a Hijaz Achough), which consists of a repeated series of two phrases, the optional variant qit'a Shahnaz, and an optional phrase leading down to the tonic. A comparison of two different Yusuf Omar performances (Amiri's transcription [1990] and the Inedit recording presented here) shows a wide scope for improvisation in the meyana. Yusuf Omar's rendition of qit'a Qazaz is also composed of two distinct ideas and features both natural and flattened qualities of 4. Qazaz and the following passage in Saba (on 8) may be preceded with a *dulab* interlude, which includes an interesting juxtaposition of phrases in Saba and Hijaz. After the passage in Saba (and the optional Hijaz Shaytani) a series of short qit'as function to provide what can be viewed as a teslim section. This section begins with an interesting option of routes out of Saba, via either Nawa (which descends directly to 1) or Husseini (which reaches 1 through the micro-qit'a Buselik) (B. Rijab 1985, 79). The teslim section continues with the two short qit'as Hijaz Madani and Nagriz. The following schematic diagram compares the representations of the maqam by Sha'oubi (abbreviated SI), Yusuf Omar (YO), and B. Rijab (BR); the umbrella central section, meyana, and teslim are indicated above their respective components.

104

	Central				Meyanas							Teslim section			
SI:	Tah/H D	Hus	Ngz	Jls	D hj	H A	Shz	D hj	Qaz	D sb	Sab	Nwa	Teslim		
YO:	Tah/H D	Hus	H D/ Ngz	Jls	D hj	H A	Shz	D sb	Qaz	D sb	Sab	Hus	Bus	HMd	Ngz
BR:	Tah/H D	Hus		Jls	D hj	H A	Shz		Qaz	Sab	H Sh	Hus/ Nwa	Bus	HMd	Ngz
	3-8-3	8-5	4-7-8-1		5-1	5'-8-1			4'-8	4'-8	3'-8-5	7-5'-8	5-8-5	3-6-1	7-4	7-7-5-1
		Hus/ 1							Bey/ 8; ♭4	Saba/8				Rast/5		
						Wahda 4/4										

Abbreviations: Bey=Beyat; Bus=Buselik; D=*dulab* (hj/hijaz or sb/saba); H A=Hijaz Achough; HD=Hijaz Diwan; HMd=Hijaz Madani; H Sh=Hijaz Shaytani; Hus=Husseini; Jls=Jalsa; Ngz=Nagriz; Nwa=Nawa; Qaz=Qazaz; Shz=Shahnaz; Tah=Tahrir

Hijaz Diwan

Yusuf Omar
(Inedit W.268006)

4. (4:53)   Husseini   (Khalwati theme)

ma   ka   na   da   'ul   hub   ma   ka   na   da   'ul   hub   ma   ka   na   da   'ul   hub   bi

la   la   nathra tan   he   ya   sa   ba   ba   ti   da   u   hu   wa   da   wa   u   hu

Husseini Meyana (5:27)

wa   fis   sa   ba   ba   ti   da   u   hu   a   a   he   he

a   ma   ka   na   da   'ul   hub   bil   lah

nath   ra   tan   hi   ya   fis   sa   ba   ba   ti   da'   u   hu

wa   da   wa   u   hu   hi   ya   fis   sa   ba   ba   ti   da'   u   hu   wa   da wa   u   hu

5. Hijaz Diwan (6:37)

ya   rah   ma   tan   ya   rah   ma   tan   ya   rah   ma

tan   lil   mu   gh ra   mi   na   wa   in   ta   kun   wa   in   ta   kun

Nagriz (7:08)

qat   la   ha   wa   ka   fa   in   na   hum   shu   ha   da   'a   hu

wau   wa

Jalsa (7:26)

a   hu   di   li   au   de

ya   dim   de   lim   ya   aun   dim   ya   dim   de   dim

ya   dim   a   fan   dim   a   fan

dim   a   fan   di   ma   di   ma   fan   di   ma

Interlude in iqa' Wahda Tawila (7:54), iqa' continues through meyana section

6. Meyana Hijaz Achough (8:18)

ya　　　　　　　le li　ya rah ma tan　　　　　lil　mu gh ra　mi na wain

ta kun　　　qat　　la ha wa　　ka fa (in na) hum　　shuha da　　'a hu

7. Shahnaz (9:03)

ya　　　　　　　　　　　　　　li a　le il

8. (9:35)

ya　　rah ma tan lil　mu ghra mi　　na wa (in)　ta kun

qat la　　ha wa ka fa　in na hum　　fa in na hum fa in na hum

Saba interlude (10:00)

shu ha da　　　'a hu

(Hijaz interlude material)

9. Qazaz (10:35)

ya rah ma tan　ya rah ma tan

ha　　ha　　akh　　wa in ta kun

qat la ha wa ka fa in na hum (fa in na hum) shu ha da 'a hu ma na man

mana ma na ma na ma na man a man a a na man a na man an

Saba interlude with allusion to Segah (11:39)   **10. Saba (12:12)**
and Hijaz interlude material (11:56)

a man a na ya we li wa na jay tu

mu hu al a wis al qa ti 'a tan

Jalsa via qit'a Husseini (12:35)

ha ke (tha) minal 'in sa fi ka na ja za 'u hu ha ke tha min al 'in sa

(fi) ka na ja za a u hu

Buselik (12:57) **Hijaz Madani**

il la ja me mao ya dust

Nagriz/teslim (13:05)

ya ya

a man

'Araibun

Kojaman notes that the two maqams 'Araibun Ajam and 'Araibun Arab are traditionally performed in succession and without an intermediary pesta (2001, 133). Sha'oubi describes a single maqam—'Araibun—as a compound structure, the first half of which ('Araibun Ajam) is in naghmah Hijaz and features classical poetry, the second ('Araibun Arab) is in naghmah Beyat with zheiri poetry (1982, 107ff). The tahrir alfaz are *Ah, wai*, and the maqam is accompanied throughout by iqa' Yugrug. Sha'oubi's generic refrain is maintained throughout the maqam but is transposed from Hijaz to Beyat as part of the larger modulation scheme. The melody of 'Araibun Arab is similar to that of Mahmudi; Sha'oubi's rendition of the sayha (section 3) evokes the atmosphere of the Persian gusheh Bayat-e Raje. The penultimate qit'a (before Ibrahimi) features a brief rhythmical melody that resembles certain manifestations of the ubiquitous qit'a Mthalatha; this dovetails with Ibrahimi and functions as a teslim.

Other qit'as listed: Hijaz Diwan, Shahnaz, Sufyan.
Qit'a I appearance in maqams: Ibrahimi, Madmi, Mathnawi, Mugabl, Nahawand, Sa'idi, Qatar

Sha'oubi Ibrahim performance:

'Araibun Ajam ⟶ 'Araibun Arab

Tah	AAj	Say	AAj	Say	Sdi	AAj	AAr	j. Seg	Bey	Bhz	Qtr	AAr	j. Seg	Bey	Ibr
7̲-4	2-4	7-4	2-4	7-4	4-1	1-4	2-4-1	4-2	6-1	6-1	5-2	4-2	4-2	4-1	1-4-1
Hijaz/1							Beyat/1				(♭5)				
Yugrug 12/4															

Abbreviations: AAj='Araibun Ajam; AAr='Araibun Arab; Bey=Beyat; Bhz=Bheirzawi; j. Seg=jins Segah; Ibr=Ibrahimi; Qtr=Qatar; Say=Sayha; Sdi=Sa'idi; Tah=Tahrir

'Araibun

Sha'oubi Ibrahim
(1982)

ma u lai

refrain in naghmah Beyat

7. Sayha   jins Segah

8. Beyat   9. Bheirzawi   10. Qatar

ma'wed

11. 'Araibun Arab   12. jins Segah   13. Beyat (in iqa')

yaba Davud ya beni

(free meter)

Ibrahimi

ah

khe   yi

Hijaz Kar

Mohammed Qubanchi's creation Hijaz Kar is set to zheiri poetry without rhythmic accompaniment; its tahrir vocable is *Ya leili*. Sha'oubi sets his performance on C and provides scales (identical to the Mashreq cognate) on G and C (1982, 82). The theme for Hijaz Kar itself consists of a main phrase (arbitrarily labelled "A" here) descending from 3' or 8 to 5, then 5/4-1; Sha'oubi's and particularly Yusuf Omar's performance (a recording available throughout 2001 at www.iraqimusic.com) of this theme highlights an 8-3' opening gesture. A cadential phrase ("B") that runs up and down the entire scale (1-8-1) is rather striking and anomalous in the traditional repertoire but occurs in another Qubanchi creation, maqam Kurd. Both "A" and "B" phrases are appended to other qit'as throughout the course of the maqam in Sha'oubi's rendition. Hakimi figures prominently through its several repetitions, juxtaposed with different qit'as. The varieties of modal modulations represented in the succession of qit'as in Sha'oubi's rendition is complicated by their unusual transpositions, which maintain the melodic outline of the qit'a while affecting a commutation of the expected intervals. In Sha'oubi's performance the qit'as Muste'ar, Mukhalef Kirkuk, and Mukhalef have tonics on C rather than the usual E♭ or B♭; Hakimi is performed with E♮ instead of E♭.

Other qit'as listed: Mugabl.

Sha'oubi Ibrahim performance:

Tahrir	Hijaz Kar	Hakimi	Hijaz Kar	Hakimi	M Krk	H Kar	Must	Hakimi	Hakimi	Mkh	H Kar	Teslim
8-3'-1	8-3'-1; 1-8-1	3'-4'-1	8-3'-1	4'-5'-3'	2'-5'-8	3'-1	3'-1	4'-5'-1	4'-5'-1	3'-8	3'-6-3'	3'-1-8-1
				(♭5')			Seg/3		(♭5')	Mkh/8		
							(♮4')					

Abbreviations: H Kar=Hijaz Kar; Mkh=Mukhalef; M Krk=Mukhalef Kirkuk; Must=Muste'ar; Seg=Segah

Hijaz Kar

Sha'oubi Ibrahim
(1982)

1. Tahrir (theme "A")

Ya   lei   li   a   leili   a

2. Hijaz Kar

leil

(theme "B"/cadence)

3. Hakimi

Hijaz Kar

4. Hakimi   **Mukhalef Kirkuk**

ayaya   ya

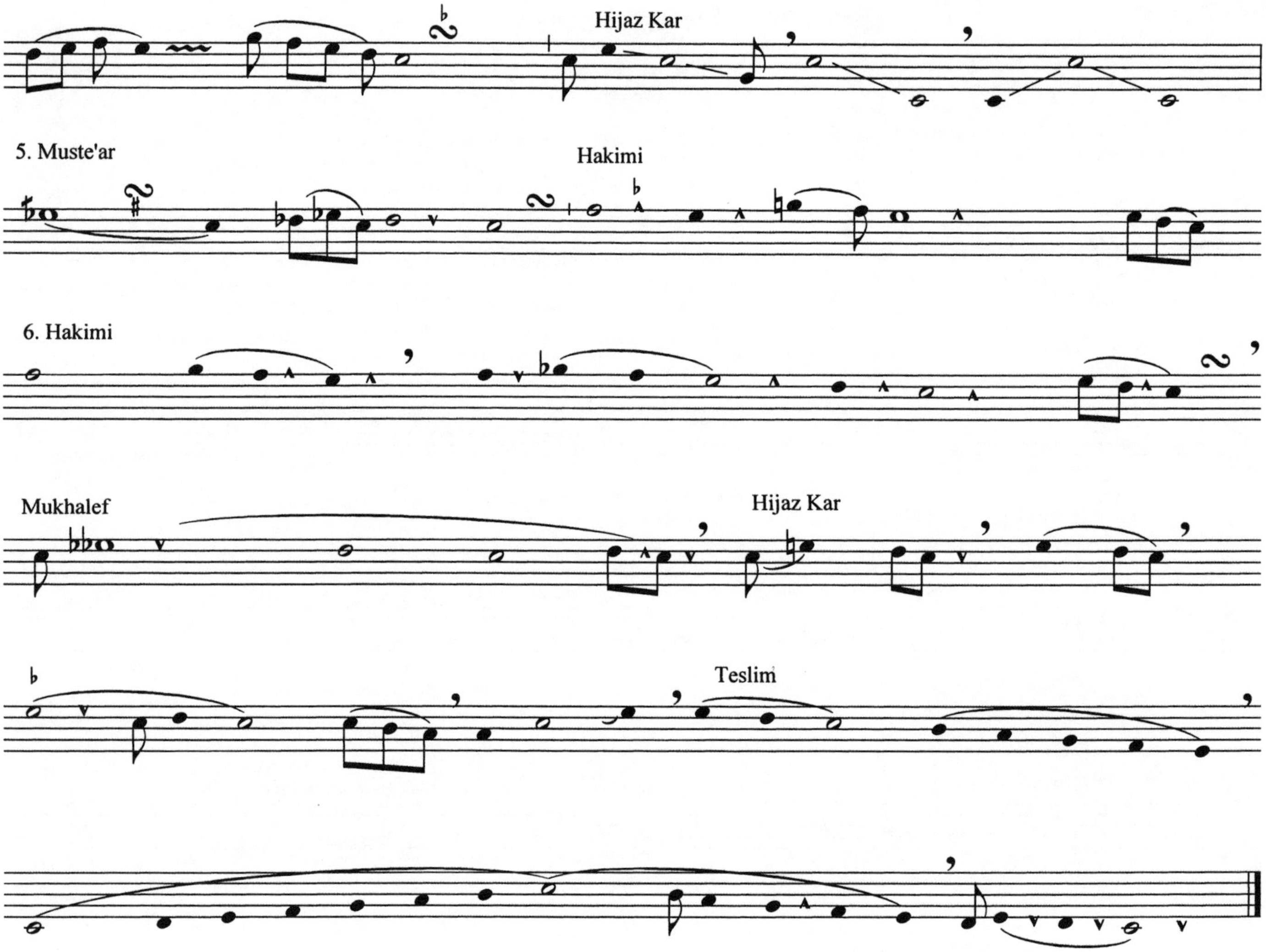
Hijaz Kar
5. Muste'ar
Hakimi
6. Hakimi
Mukhalef
Hijaz Kar
Teslim

Homayun

Imported from Iran and adapted by Mohammed Qubanchi, Homayun is set to classical Arabic and has no rhythmic accompaniment, meyana, or teslim. Sha'oubi uses the tahrir alfaz *Ah, yaba*; Hamid al-Saadi *Aman janem ya daday*. The Iraqi incarnation draws upon the Persian daramad but differs in the treatment of 2, which is flattened here (although Sha'oubi occasionally performs this closer to the original *koron*/kar bimol; his intonation of 3 is often flat as well) and is not melodically polarized. Qit'a Hijaz Diwan extends the range of the maqam and functions somewhat like the gusheh Bidad (polarizing 5), which is the most definitive modulation in Persian Homayun. Qazaz features a change of scale that somewhat parallels gusheh 'Ushshaq/Oj in the Persian modulation scheme; it occurs in the tonic register in the Iraqi maqam (rather than the upper, as in Iran). Hijaz Gharib presents the definitive 4-1 Hijaz progression.

Other qit'a listed: Huizawi.
Qit'a I appearance in maqams: Hleilawi, Jamal, Mathnawi.

Sha'oubi Ibrahim performance:

Homayun strophe	Hijaz Diwan	Homayun	Hijaz Gharib	Qazaz	Homayun
7-1-3-1	5-7-1	1-3-1	4-1	4-5-1	7-1-3-1
	(b6)			Beyat/1	

Homayun

Sha'oubi Ibrahim
(1982)

1. Tahrir

Ah   ya   ba ya ba

(joze allusion to Persian Homayun)   2. Homayun

3. Homayun

4. Homayun

5. Homayun   6. Homayun

7. Hijaz Diwan

Homayun

8. Hijaz Gharib

9. Hijaz Gharib

10. Beyat/Qazaz

11. Homayun

12. Homayun

ba   be

ba   be ba   be

Huizawi

Huizawi is set to classical poetry and has no iqa', tahrir (it begins with Huizawi and the first couplet of poetry), or meyana. The tune is a very static polarization of 4 with neighbor-note decorations, similar in character to Mathnawi; the teslim is similar to that of maqam Madmi. Qit'a Dasht provides a contrast of range and scale.

Other qit'as listed: Madmi, Mathnawi, 'Araibun Ajam, Lami, Nahawand, Qazaz, Mukhalef Kirkuk.
Qit'a I appearance in maqams: Homayun, Jamal, Madmi.

Sha'oubi Ibrahim performance:

Huizawi	Sa'idi	Huizawi	Dasht	Hijaz Gharib	Huizawi	Huizawi	Teslim
4; 4-1	6-4-1	4	3-5-7-1	5-1-3	5-3	4	4-1; 1-5-6-1
			Husseini/1 (♭5)				(♮6)

Huizawi

Sha'oubi Ibrahim
(1982)

1. Huizawi

2. Huizawi   3. Huizawi

4. Huizawi   5. Sa'idi

6. Huizawi   7. Huizawi   Dasht

8. Hijaz Gharib

9. Huizawi

Teslim

say   ib   khey   ib   ya   gal   bi   ah

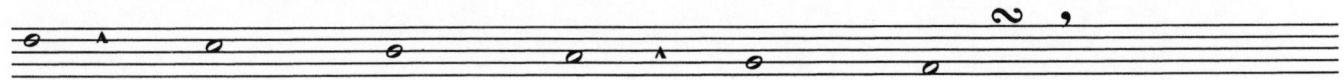

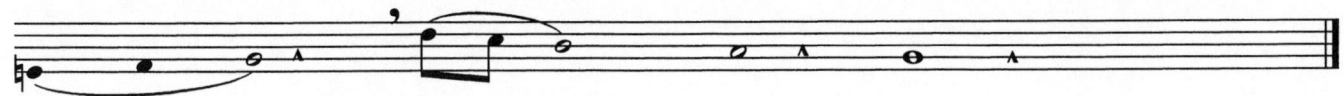

ah

Madmi

Madmi features zheiri poetry, is accompanied continuously by iqa' Yugrug and has neither meyana nor jalsa. Hamid al-Saadi uses the tahrir alfaz *Ay welak yaba ya 'eyuni.* The scale of Hijaz is maintained throughout the maqam in Sha'oubi's and Qundarchi's renditions, with qit'as providing melodic variety to the main mode; the teslim is similar to that of Huizawi. Qubanchi's performances regularly include an unidentified qit'a (Bheirzawi?) that modulates to Beyat/1. As the tahrir is clipped in my copy of Sha'oubi, I have included tahrirs of Qundarchi (ALCD 183) and Qubanchi (available at iraqimusic.com throughout 2002).

Other qit'as listed: Bheirzawi, Huizawi, Nahawand.
Qit'a I appearances in maqam: Hadidi, Mathnawi, Mugabl.

Sha'oubi Ibrahim performance:

Tahrir	Madmi	Sa'idi	Madmi	'Araibun Ajam	Hijaz Gharib	Madmi	Teslim
4-2; 4-7-2	5-2	4-1	5-7-2	7-5-3	1-4	5-7-4	5-1-6-1

Yugrug 12/4

Madmi

Refrain
"tunraround" or tacit
Tahrir (Rashid Qundarchi on ALCD 183)
Yu na ya na a ya ??
Tahrir (Mohammed Qubanchi at www.iraqimusic.com)
Yu na yu na wela ya ba ya ba ya 'eyu ni
Madmi (henceforth Sha'oubi Ibrahim 1982)
Madmi
Sa'idi
Madmi
'Araibun Ajam
Ah
Hijaz Gharib
Madmi
Teslim
yu be yu be yu be yu be yu be yube
yu be yu be yu be yu be

Qatar

Composed by Mohammed Qubanchi, Qatar is set to zheiri poetry and uses the tahrir alfaz *Ya, leilem, leil.* It has no iqa' or meyana. The structure of the maqam has nothing in common with the Persian gusheh Qatar in avaz Bayat-e Tork or the Kurdish maqam of the same name. As perfomed by Sha'oubi, Qatar presents some fundamental problems: unreliable intonation and qit'as listed in the text that are not apparent or are extremely abbreviated in his recording. He regularly sings ♭3 while playing a ♮3 on the joze, and the intonation 2 is rather sharp (thereby alluding to jins Beyat rather than the prescribed Hijaz [Sha'oubi 1982, 53]). Two gestures characterize the melody of Qatar: a double neighbor decoration of 1 that descends to 7 or 6 and a 4-1 descent (which Sha'oubi clearly intones in Hijaz) that eventually cadences on 7. The tendency to cadence on 7 led Bilal to conclude that the naghmah for Qatar is actually Nikris (Kojaman 2001, 149). Al-Basri's transcription of the main theme of Qatar (1996, 212) is essentially double-neighbor decoration of 1, ending on 7.

Mthalatha is listed but appears virtually identical to Sha'oubi's standard closing phrase. Homayun is listed as following 'Araibun Ajam (the latter is simply a prolongation of 4), but actually repeats earlier phrases from Qatar with ♮3; the progressions for Qatar and Homayun are indeed similar, both featuring a core of 1-3-1. Any sense of contrast provided by qit'as as performed by Sha'oubi is minimal, creating the effect of a strophic maqam. The teslim phrase quickly follows (with a return to ♭3) double-neighbor motion around the tonic (that evokes Homayun) and a final descent to ♮6.

Qit'a I appearances in maqams: Bajalan, Bheirzawi, Hleilawi, Ibrahimi, Juburi, Mugabl, Sharqi Rast.

Sha'oubi Ibrahim performance:

Tahrir	Qatar	Qatar	Mthalatha	Qatar	'Araibun Ajam	Homayun	Teslim
1-3-7	6-3-6; 1-4-6	1-4-6	2-6	1-3-6	4-3	7-3-7	1-3-6

Qatar

Sha'oubi Ibrahim
(1982)

Other Hijaz Maqams

Sources provide some insight into the more obscure maqams in the large Hijaz family through their appearance as type I qit'as; al-Basri also provides transcriptions of tahrir/bedwa themes (1996, 212–14). Qit'a components for these maqams are listed in table 1.3 above; most are simply structured and lack meyanas. Al-Basri sets four on G (Hijaz Gharib, Mathnawi, Hijaz Shaytani, Jamal) and five on D (Hijaz Achough, Beyat Ajam, 'Araibun Ajam,'Ushaish). The inclusion of 'Ushaish is anomalous, as it appears consistently in naghmah Beyat throughout the repertoire in other sources. Most of the themes of these maqams are variations on the definitive Hijaz feature of polarizing 4 and descending to 1 (Sa'idi, Hijaz Gharib, Mathnawi, Jamal, 'Ushaish). Beyat Ajam descends directly 4-1 without this prolongation, 'Araibun Arab features a 1-4-1 profile (cf., Sha'oubi's rendition in 'Araibun Ajam that features a Beyat modality), and Hijaz Achough a double descent of 4-1-4-1. Al-Basri's transcription of Hijaz Shaytani mixes Beyat and Hijaz tetrachords, a feature not found in its appearance as a type I qit'a in the sources for maqam Hijaz Diwan. The following transcriptions are taken from al-Basri (1996) with the exception of Sa'idi, which is from various qit'a I manifestations in Sha'oubi. Here Sa'idi's prolongation of 4 takes the form of successive 4-3-2 descents, an idiomatic feature of international Hijaz.

Other Hijaz Family Maqams

Themes according to al-Basri (1996)

Hijaz Gharib

'Araibun Ajam

Mathnawi

Hijaz Achough

Hijaz Shaytani

Beyat Ajam

Jamal

'Ushaish (N.B., appears throughout the repertoire as a qit'a I in naghmah Beyat)

Sa'idi as qit'a I in Sha'oubi Ibrahim (1982)

in maqam Madmi

in maqam Huizawi

in maqam 'Araibun

5

The Saba Family

Saba

Saba is sung in classical Arabic, uses the tahrir vocables *Ah, wai* and lacks rhythmic accompaniment (with the exception of iqa' Wahda in the prescribed *dulab* before the meyana). Saba is a simply structured maqam and there is a general consensus in the sources regarding its main components: Sayha Mahmudi and a short rendition of Aboush for the meyana, followed by Jahargah (identified as Khalwati by B. Rijab [1985]) before the teslim. Sha'oubi and Amiri include the qit'a Awshar, which Sha'oubi identifies as a short descending phrase with altered scale degrees (♮2-1-7, ending on ♭6, i.e., the naghmah Bastenegar) occurring well before the jalsa (1982, 105); a similar phrase appears again before the teslim of Sha'oubi. Amiri's designation of Awshar (1990, 178) is not clearly identified in his transcription of Yusuf Omar's performance; the parallel location to Sha'oubi's placement (1990, 184–85) includes ♮2 but the contour and content of the phrase is rather different. Jahargah is not clearly evident following the meyana in the Yusuf Omar transcription; there are some seemingly anomalous pitches (♯7, ♯6, and ♮2, alluding to Nahawand/1) and the repetition of a wide-ranging phrase (7-1) not found in other sources.

Appearance as qit'a I in maqams: Ajam, Jahargah, Husseini, Hijaz Diwan, Mansuri, Rashdi, Taher.

Sha'oubi Ibrahim performance:

Tahrir	Saba	Saba	Awshar	Saba	Jalsa	Interlude	S Mah	Aboush	Saba	Jhg	Saba	Tes
3-♭6-1	3-4-1	3-1	2-♭6	3-5-1	5-1	3-4-1	4	4-1	3-5-1	5-7-3	3-1	4-1
			Seg/♭6					Beyat/1		Jhg/3		
					Wda 4/4							

Abbreviations: Jhg=Jahargah; Seg=Segah; S Mah=Sayha Mahmudi; Tes=Teslim; Wda=Wahda

Saba

Sha'oubi Ibrahim
(1982)

1. Tahrir

Ah

2. Saba   **3. Saba**   Awshar

4. Saba   **5. Saba**

6. Saba   **7. Saba**

jalsa

ya   leili   a   lil   ya   leili   a   leili

instrumental interlude in iqa' Wahda

(iqa' stops)

8. Sayha Mahmudi   Aboush   **9. Saba**

ah

Jahargah   10. Jahargah

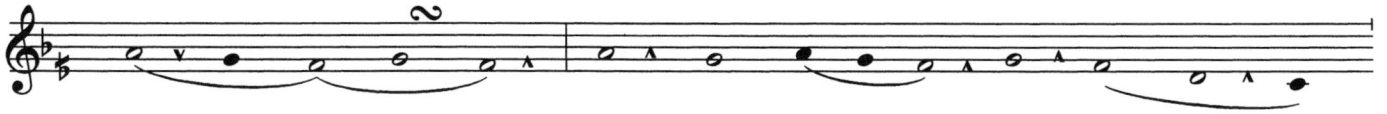

                   (Saba)   11. Saba

Teslim

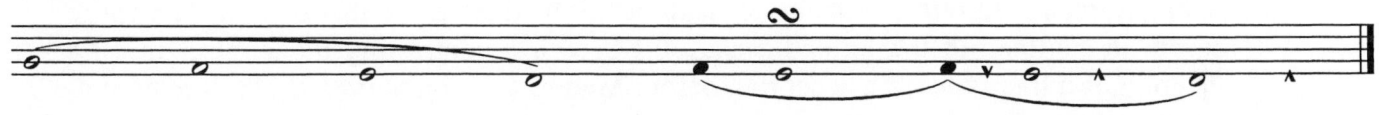

ah

Hadidi

Hadidi is set to zheiri poetry, employs the tahrir alfaz *La bila, galbak wa galbi ya 'eyuni*, and is accompanied throughout by iqa' Yugrug; it has no meyana. As performed by Sha'oubi, Hadidi itself is a narrow 3-2-1 melody that only touches on 4 ornamentally, thereby evoking more of the feel of a Beyat tetrachord (particularly bringing to mind Persian Shur). This effect is reinforced by a group of qit'as which form a decisive shift to naghmah Beyat; the refrain remains in naghmah Saba throughout this section. The entire maqam is confined to the limited range of 1-5 with a contrasting modal shift in qit'a Madmi. Qit'a Iraq is listed as occuring before Madmi (Sha'oubi 1982, 57) but is not apparent in the performance. The maqam ends with a clear establishment of Saba by means of qit'a Mthalatha (transposed to the scale of Saba) and a cadential phrase that is recycled from maqam Saba featuring the alfaz *yuba, yuba ya 'eyuni*.

Other qit'as listed: Mansuri.

Sha'oubi Ibrahim performance:

Tahrir	Hadidi	S Mah	Aboush	Mugabl	Hadidi	O Gl	Qbsh	Had	Had	(Iraq)	Madmi	Had	Mth	Tes
4-1	4-1	4	4-1	5-1	3-1	4-1	5-1	4-1	5-1	?	4-2	5-1	1-4-1	5-1
			Beyat/1			Beyat/1					Hijaz/1			

Yugrug 12/4

Abbreviations: Had=Hadidi; Mth=Mthalatha; O Gl='Omar Gala; Qbsh=Qariabash; S Mah=Sayha Mahmudi; Tes=Teslim

Hadidi

Sha'oubi Ibrahim
(1982)

Refrain

Refrain fragment

1. Tahrir

La bila

galbak wa galbi ya 'eyuni

2. Hadidi

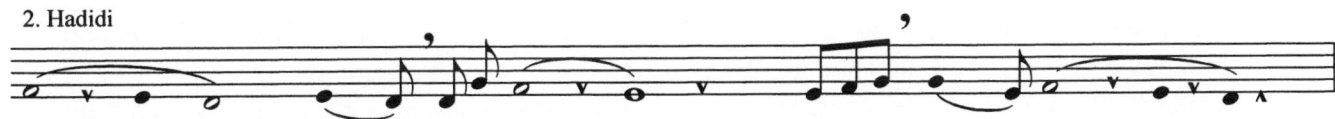

3. Sayha Mahmudi

Aboush

4. Mugabl

Ah

mena weil

5. Hadidi

'Omar Gala

Qariabash

alulalu

babe

babeheiran

6. Hadidi

7. Hadidi

('Iraq?)

Madmi

Hadidi

Mthalatha

o ya   ha lal

le

"Teslim"

yu ba

'eyu

ni

Mansuri

Maqam Mansuri is set to classical Arabic poetry and is accompanied by two iqa's: beginning in Samah and shifting to Yugrug after the first meyana. Sha'oubi uses the tahrir alfaz *Aye*; Hamid al-Saadi, *Aray, janem, ay baba, way.* According to Scheherazade Hassan, Mansuri "far exceeds" Saba in importance (1995a, 22); its structure is more complex and akin to the "big" *asliyah* maqams (Rast, Segah, and Hijaz Diwan) than it is to Saba, its short and relatively simple parent. Indeed, Mansuri is an important maqam in a more general view of the Iraqi repertoire as a whole: it appears on many recordings and is the only maqam with alternate takes available on international commercial releases (Yusuf Omar on Philips 6586006 and Inedit 260063). H. Rijab (1983, 88) maintains that the name Mansuri derives from the large Mansur ney (in G, the standard size Turkish ney) as distinct from the standard ney (in C) of the Arab tradition. As a maqam, the name is not found in the Turkish-Mashreqi tradition; it has nothing in common with the Persian gusheh Mansuri of dastgah Chahargah. While the scale of Mansuri is that of Saba on G, it has individual qualities that differentiate it from Saba: the tahrir outlines a downward arc 1-5-1 (compared to Saba's 3-6-3-1), and it idiomatically juxtaposes phrases in Beyat (on the same tonic pitch G). Sha'oubi and Yusuf Omar repeat this latter compound feature strophically (it appears only once in the Qundarchi example transcribed). Sha'oubi includes the micro-qit'a Nahoft to conclude the Beyat portion of the phrase before the jalsa. Yusuf Omar's Beyat phrase begins higher (on F) and stresses C. The first meyana in the version of Sha'oubi begins nominally in Husseini (on 5, though its exposition is not as clear as other qit'a I transpositions) followed by Rast on 4. The parallel passage (based on musical contents and ordinal position in the scheme of the maqam) in Yusuf Omar's performance is simply described as Beyat (Scheherazade Hassan 1995a, 23). Qundarchi's two meyanas are virtually identical renditions of Husseini. Arwah appears after the second meyana in Sha'oubi and Qundarchi but is not apparent in Yusuf Omar's performance.

Other qit'as listed: Aboush, Hijaz Gharib, Mukhalef, Saba.
Qit'a I appearances in maqams: Hadidi, Ibrahimi, Khanabat, Panjgah, Rast, Segah.

Rashid Qundarchi performance:

Tahrir	Mansuri	Beyat	Jalsa	Mey/Husseini		Mathnawi	Meyana	Arwah	Mthalatha	Teslim
1-5-3-1	3-1	4-1	3-1	8-5	7-1	4-1	8-5	5-7-5	5-7-1: 5-1	8-1
		Beyat/1		Husseini/1		Hijaz/1	Husseini/1		Beyat/1	
Samah 36/4				Yugrug 12/4						

Mansuri

Rashid Qundarchi
(Al-Sur ALCD 183)

3. Meyana/Husseini (1:54)

a   i   a   i   a

(Rast)

a   (??)

a man   a

man   a man   a man   a man   a man   a man

iqa' Yugrug (instrumental)   4. Mathnawi (2:47)

ya

ya

(??)   *(??)*

a man a man   a la

a   man   a

ya   wa   wa   wa wa wan   bi dad   bi da   dam

instrumental   5. Meyana (3:46)

ah   a   a

(??)

Arwah (4:09)

(??)

6

(??)

Mthalatha (4:25)

Bor   dem   jur   ye   lei

3   3

ba   ba   ba   ba   ba

6. Mthalatha (4:47)

a   a   man   (??)

ba   ba   3

(another voice?)   Teslim (5:15)

ah

6

The Segah Family

Sources present interesting variations and particular problems for defining the modal properties of the Segah family. Segah maqams have a predeliction for including the qit'as Mukhalef Kirkuk and Qaderbijan.

Segah

Segah is a complex maqam set to classical Arabic poetry, the tahrir alfaz *Alila aman bidaday* and two iqa's: beginning with Samah and shifting (via a new *dulab*) to Yugrug before the meyanas (cf., maqams Mansuri and Nawa). Segah in the Iraqi tradition is characterized by an essential ambiguity of structure and nomenclature concerning two alternate definitions: Segah proper, as the third octave species of Rast, and Hozzam, as the ♭6 species of Hijaz. I have encountered the same confusing and inconsistent overlap among musicians in both Morocco and Syria as well. Sha'oubi (1982, 66) entitles the maqam "Segah al-Iraqi," denoting some kind of special differentiation from the Pan-maqam tradition. B. Rijab prefers to name the maqam Hozzam and lists scales for both Hozzam and Segah, the latter with ascending (♭5) and descending (♭5) forms (1985, 59).

The contents of the maqam reflect this duality, though in a manner that is not entirely consistent in the sources—the tahrir of B. Rijab is set in Hozzam (1985, 62–63), while Sha'oubi and Yusuf Omar use Segah. The long final qit'a, Jamal, is in Hijaz/3 (phrased to evoke Nahawand/6) which pivots through Hozzam en route to the teslim. The most striking feature of Segah is its large meyana section, which consists of an extended succession of short, closely related qit'as. Consolidating functionally related qit'as, a general view of the maqam could be represented in four main sections as:

I		II				III			IV	
Tahrir/bedwa/Jasas	Segah	Mansuri	Bastenegar	Jalsa	Dulab	Meyanas			Jamal	Teslim
1-5-1; 3-5-1		3-6-3	3-1	6-1		8-4'-8		8-1-4'-8	8-5-3	6-1-6-1
		Saba/3							Hijaz/3	
Samah 36/4					Yugrug 12/4					

Sources present a wide variety of materials for section I. They all begin with qit'a Jasas (in the Turkish-Mashreqi maqam scale of Iraq); B. Rijab includes qit'as Awshar (with a ♭3 allusion to Mukhalef), Aboush, and Segah Halab. Kojaman maintains that short phrase of Awshar and Hakimi may be inserted into the opening verses sung in Segah after the tahrir (2001, 211). Yusuf Omar's section I emphasizes allusions to Beyat/3, which descend to 1. Section II material repeats phrases in Mansuri and then descends to 1 of Segah before the jalsa, thereby evoking Bastenegar (and is listed as such by Sha'oubi [1982, 67]; B. Rijab labels the jalsa as Segah Ajam [1985, 64]).

As the sources present a variety of orderings and musical contents, the long meyana section (III) can be performed in various ways: Segah Balban, with the possible attachment of Sufyan (which Kojaman considers as the second meyana [2001, 212]), descends back to 1, creating a natural division. B. Rijab further emphasizes this by recapitulating the entire tahrir section here (1985, 65–66). Hakimi, Mthalatha, Mukhalef Kirkuk, Sunbule, and Tiflis, in various configurations, form another block of meyana material, which prolongs the apogee and features alternate pitches along with subtly shifting tetrachord focuses (Sunbule briefly alludes to Mukhalef). Salmak in B. Rijab alludes to Beyat/3' and includes a passing ♮4. The ambitus of this block of qit'as focuses on 4'-8, exemplified by Yusuf Omar's performance.

According to B. Rijab (1985, 68–69), Jamal (section IV here) can be approached by one of three linking passes, the first of which is used by both Sha'oubi and Yusuf Omar (the third is a glimpse of the rare maqam Bajalan, in the form of a qit'a I transposition). Jamal leads smoothly to the teslim. The following list compares the ordering of each section of components by Sha'oubi (abbreviated SI), B. Rijab (BR), and Yusuf Omar (YO). The nature of the variation and inconsistency evident here is very much akin to that found in various radif sources.

Section I

SI: Jasas, Segah
BR: Tahrir, Jasas, Awshar, Segah Halab, Segah
YO: Jasas, Segah

Section II

Mansuri, Bastenegar, jalsa
Mansuri, Segah Ajam
Mansuri, Bastenegar, Segah Ajam/jalsa

Section IIIa

SI: Segah Balban, Sufyan, Mthalatha
BR: Segah Balban, Sufyan, recap section I
YO: Segah Balban, jalsa

Section IIIb

Hakimi, Mukhalef Kirkuk, Sunbule, Mukhalef, Tiflis, Jamal, Teslim
Mukhalef Kirkuk, Hakimi, Mthalatha, Salmak, Sunbule, Tiflis
Sufyan, Hakimi, Mthalatha, Mukhalef Kirkuk, Sunbule, Tiflis

Section IV

SI: Jamal, Teslim
BR: three different links to Jamal, Jamal, Nahoft, Segah Ajam
YO: link to Jamal, Jamal, Nahoft, Segah Ajam/Teslim

Segah

Yusuf Omar
(Ocora C.580066)

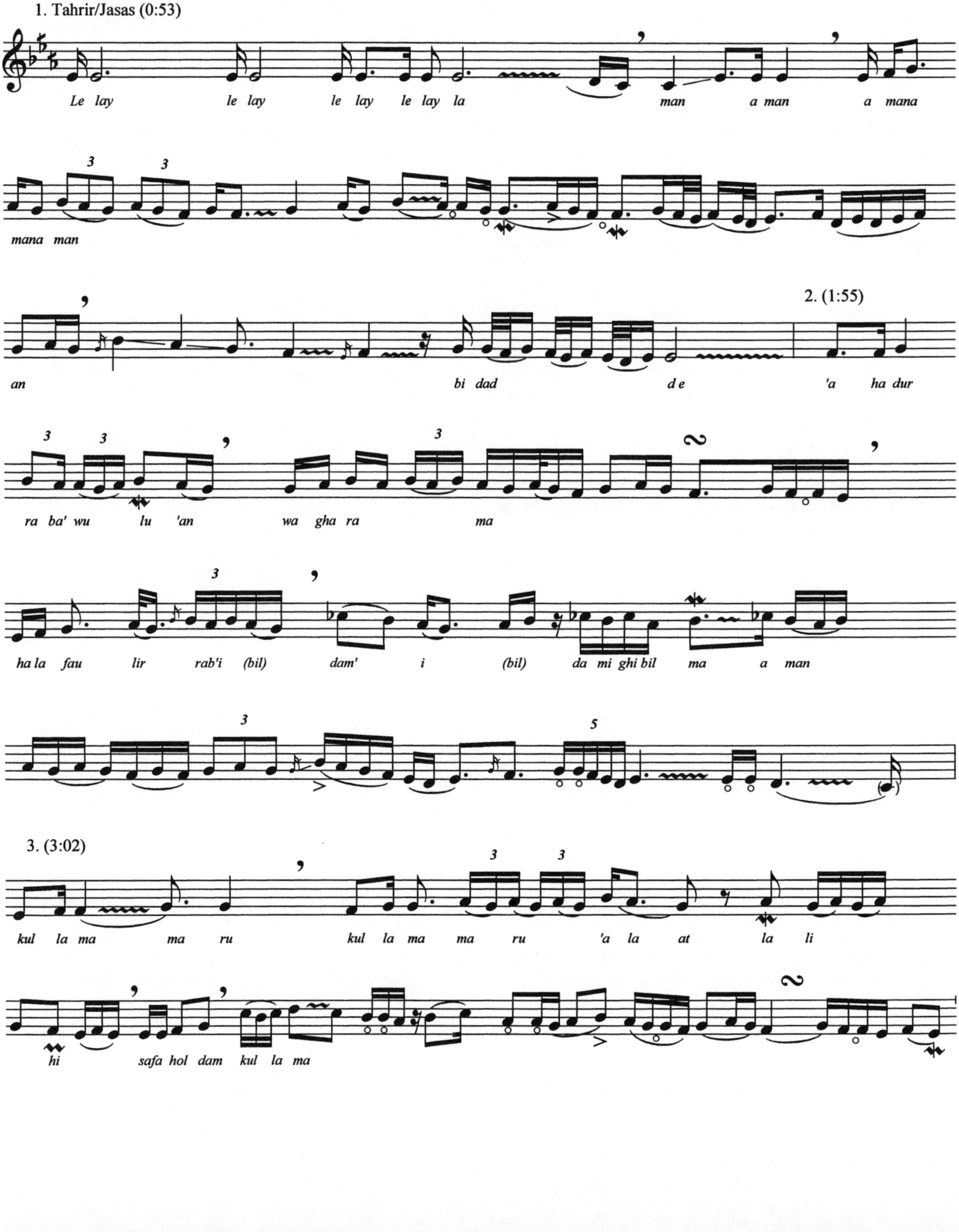

ma ru'al lat la li   sa fa hol dam`a gha bi dil sif hin si ja ma

a

4. Mansuri (4:37)

kul la ma   na hat ha ma   ma tu li wa

fi a ra kil shir a   na wah tul ha ma   a

ma   eh

5. Mansuri (5:28)

o eh kul la ma na hat ha ma ma tu li wa

jins Beyat (5:45)

fi a rak i sho bi na wa tul ha ma ma   ah

ya na da ma ya fu 'a di 'an ta kum

ma   fa 'al   tum   bi fu 'a   di   ya   na da   ma

ya   na   da   eh

6. Mansuri (6:38)

ya   na   da   ma   ya fu 'a

di 'an   da kum   ma   fa 'al   tum   bi fu 'a   di

ya   na   da   ma

Jalsa/Segah 'Ajam (7:02)

eh da   bi dad   bi dad   bi dad   bi dad

a   bi dad   de

Refrain in iqa' Yugrug (7:24)

generic refrain theme

7. Segah Balban (7:47)

ya da   a   ha

8. (8:13)

a   man   ya   na   da   ma   ya   fu 'a   di'in   da kum

ma   fa 'al   tum   bi   fu 'a   di   ya   na   da   ma

ma   fa 'al   tum   bi   fu 'a   di   ya   na   da

a

o

9. Sufyan (9:23)   Hakimi? (9:38)

na za li   3   3   *li   man*   *ma   a'lay*

kum sa   da ti   min ha   ra   jin   lau ta rud   dun   na   la

li   nal   qo da   ma   ya   ba ya   ba   ya   baha na yi in a i ya ha

10. Sayha Hakimi? (10:39)

ah   ah

a   man

11. Mthalatha (11:05)

ay   ba   ba   ba   ba   ya   ba   ha

12. Mukhalef Kirkuk (11:38)

a   ya   ya   ya   ya   ya   ya   ya   a

(joze Awj muhasiba)

ya   ya   ya

13. Sunbule/Salmak (12:19)

ru   mad   re   mad   ru   mad   ru   mad   ru   mad   wa   sih

(Sunbule?) (12:33)

toj   a   man   (chi)   to   ja   n i   ru   mad   wa

sih   wa   ja   ni   'e   yun

Lyrics under staves:

toj u' nl toj anni i a

Tiflis? (12:52)

ma a' lay kum sa da ti min ha ra jin lau ta ru du na la ya li nal ku da

a

Tiflis

a man al a kh a i wa

Jamal link (13:17)

a

Jamal (13:25)

ma a' lai kum sa da ti min ha ra jin

lau ta rud dun na la ya li nal qo da

14. Jamal (13:55)

in ta nat in ta nat da ru

na da ri kum fa tha ku rul ha h da wa

zu ru na ma na ma in ta nat

da ra na an da ri kum fath kurul ha da wa zu ru na ma na a

(14:37)

al' law yu ba

al' law yu ba sha lao wen wen ir ha lao

(14:59)

wen welao a man

Nahoft

a man a man a man a man a man he dau

Teslim/Segah 'Ajam (15:16)

a bi dad bi dad bi dad bi dad bi dad de

Awj

Awj is set to classical Arabic poetry and has no meyana or rhythmic accompaniment. Sha'oubi uses the tahrir alfaz *Ya lil, ah, ya lil*; Hamid al-Saadi *Ya dost*. Awj shares some characteristics with the Turkish makam Evc (e.g., its scale and descending melodic progression from 8). The main melodic activity occurs in the range of a fifth above the upper tonic; the qarar expands the range of Awj considerably, in a fashion similar to the 'Usheiran "tag-on" endings of Ajam and Husseini. Yusuf Omar's rendition (a bootleg recording from the early 1970s) sounds strikingly similar to the atmosphere of Persian Chahargah. Some characteristic motifs of Awj include a cadential figure 8-7-6-2'-8 and a 8-3' leaping gesture; Yusuf Omar's tahrir features a 3'-8 descent, with later phrases in Awj descending 4' or 5'-8.

In Sha'oubi's performance, a jalsa effect is created by the joze descending through a Hijaz/3 tetrachord to the qarar (B♭), after which the following Qaderbijan seems like a meyana. Qaderbijan, an apparently optional qit'a (absent in Yusuf Omar and Mohammed Qubanchi's performances [the latter in al-Amiri 1990, 210–12]), effects a shift to naghmah Rahat Arwah (i.e., Hozzam transposed to the pitch Iraq), although the intonation of Sha'oubi's performance is inaccurate. Sha'oubi repeats the descending gesture of Qaderbijan after the last appearance of Awj. Qit'a 'Ushshaq (which Sha'oubi maintains is a nisnomer [1982, 47]) presents a contrasting modal shift to jins Nahawand on 6, affecting a lowering of Awj's upper tonic from B♭ to B♭ (now functioning as ♭3 of Nahawand/6). Sha'oubi identifies this tetrachord as Beyat (1982, 47) but sings it closer to Nahawand; al-Amiri corroborates the use of Nahwand. The teslim appended to Ushshaq features beautiful chromatic variations, alluding to Iraq/1 and then Rahat Arwah/1. The Yusuf Omar performance consulted includes a jalsa midway through the performance that descents to the qarar; he omits qit'as Mukhalef Kirkuk and Qaderbijan.

Other qit'as listed: Arwah, Mukhalef.

Sha'oubi Ibrahim performance:

Tah	Awj	Suf	Hak	Hak	Awj	Must	Hak	Awj	M Krk	Qar	Qdj	Awj	(Qdj)	"Ush"	Tes
8-5-8	8-5'-8	4'-8	5'-8	4'	3'-6-8	3'-8	4'-8	4'-5-8	4'-8	8-1	6'-6-8	4'-6	6'-6-8	2'-3'-6	6-8-1
♯5						♯2'				R A/1	♯5',♭4'		♯5',♭4'	Nah/6	R A/1

Abbreviations: Hak=Hakimi; Must=Muste'ar; M Krk=Mukhalef Kirkuk; Nah=Nahawand; Qar=Qarar; Qdj=Qaderbijan; R A=Rahat Arwah; Suf=Sufyan; Tah=Tahrir; Tes=Teslim; Ush='Ushshaq

Awj

Sha'oubi Ibrahim
(1982)

Mukhalef Kirkuk

ayaya

joze interlude/Qarar (Rahat Arwah)

7. Qaderbijan

ya   lil   ya

ya   *lil*

8. Awj

(cf., Qaderbijan above)

ya   lil   ya   lil

"Ushshaq"   Awj/Teslim

ashtakiliman   *ya*   *ya*

(Rahat Arwah)

ya   *ya*   *ya*

ya   lil

Awshar

Awshar is set to classical Arabic poetry, employs the tahrir alfaz *Ah, ayi* (Sha'oubi) or *Ooy ay ya 'Ali jan* (H. al-Saadi), and lacks rhythmic accompaniment. Tsuge (1972, 62) and H. Rijab (1983, 196n1) mention a connection with the Persian avaz Afshari, which is possible but not as readily apparent as with other cognate modes that exist in these traditions. The scale is similar (although 4 in Afshari is a variable *koron*/natural, whereas Awshar's 4 is flat), as is the profile, which opens with 6, polarizes 3 and cadences on 1. Awshar is a strophic maqam with two contrasting ideas, arbitrarily labelled here as "A" (3-1, usually prefixed by a 1-3 leap) and "B" (5-3-1). In section five of the Sha'oubi version the ordering of the phrases are reversed ("BBA"). Qit'a Mansuri in Sha'oubi is very subtle, identical to the "B" phrase with a mere flattened mordent to 5. The meyana consists of the "A" phrase set an octave higher; the "B" phrase functions as the teslim.

Other qit'a listed: Mukhalef.
Qit'a I appearances in maqams: Khanabat, Saba, Segah.

Sha'oubi Ibrahim performance:

Tahrir	Awshar	Awshar	Mansuri	Mansuri	Awshar	Meyana	Descent	Awshar/Teslim
6-4-1	6-5-1	2-5-3	5-1	5-1	5-1	8-3'-8	3'-1	1-5-1
			(Saba/3)				(♮4, ♮5, ♯7)	

Awshar

Sha'oubi Ibrahim
(1982)

"descent"

7. Awshar/Teslim

Hakimi

Hakimi is set to zheiri poetry in iqa' Yugrug, features tahrir alfaz *Yalalia, yaba* and has no teslim or meyana. Recordings by Sha'oubi, Yusuf Omar (a bootleg recording from Iraqi television in the early 1970s), and Hamid al-Saadi (EM CD 002) vary because of options exercised by the reciters in their particular performances of this free maqam. As with maqam Awj, Yusuf Omar's brilliant rendition evokes the Persian Chahargah (particularly the gusheh Zabol in this case). The melody of Hakimi itself is remarkably narrow, focussing for the most part on 4 and characteristically ending with a quick descent to 1.

Sha'oubi's intonation in performance does not always correspond to the descriptive notes of the text, particularly his rendition of qit'a Qaderbijan and the section that follows it. In both Sha'oubi's description (1982, 26) and that of B. Rijab (1985, 25), Qaderbijan is clearly in the scale of Hozzam, with a taste of Mukhalef near the end (2-♭3-2-1); Sha'oubi ends on 3, thereby evoking Saba. I have adjusted these presumed errors in the transcription. Sha'oubi describes the following section as being in Hozzam (1982, 26) but his performance is actually an integral phrase of Hakimi itself, with the poignant G♭ as an optional intonation for 6.

The wistful qit'a Rukbani originates from Iraqi folk music and is restated strophically through several lines of text. While the iqa' continues through Sha'oubi's and Hamid al-Saadi's renditions of Rukbani, Yusuf Omar performs it without the iqa'. Sha'oubi's version alludes to Jahargah/2, turning back to the tonic with a cadential A♯ and includes a brief taste of Mukhalef with the final reestablishment of Hakimi.

Other qit'as listed: Mugabl.
Qit'a I appearances in maqams: Awj, Hijaz Kar, Segah, Tiflis.

Sha'oubi Ibrahim performance:

Tahrir	Hak	Hak	M Krk	Qdj	"Hoz"	Hak	Hak	Rukbani strophe	Hak	Mkh	Hak
3-1	4-5-1	4-5-3	2-4-1	6-3	3-6-3	3-6-1	4-6-<u>6</u>	<u>6</u>-4-1	4-1	3-1	3-1
		♭6	♭5	Hjz/3 (♮5, ♭6)	Hjz/3		(♭6)	♮<u>7</u>		♭3	

Yugrug 12/4

Abbreviations: Hak=Hakimi; Hjz=Hijaz; Hoz=Hozzam; M Krk=Mukhalef Kirkuk; Mkh= Mukhalef; Qdj=Qaderbijan

Hakimi

Sha'oubi Ibrahim
(1982)

Refrain

"turnaround" or tacit

1. Tahrir

Ya la   li   a   la   li   ah

2. Hakimi

ya   ba   ya   ba   ah

3. Hakimi

Mukhalef Kirkuk

a ya ya

4. Qaderbijan

5. ("Hozzam")

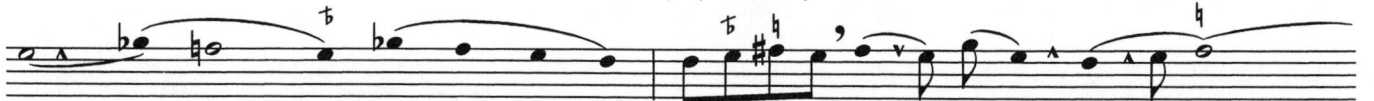

Hakimi

6. Hakimi

intro to Rukbani

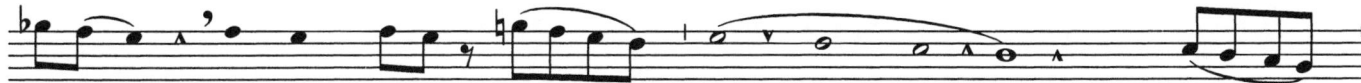

Rukbani strophe

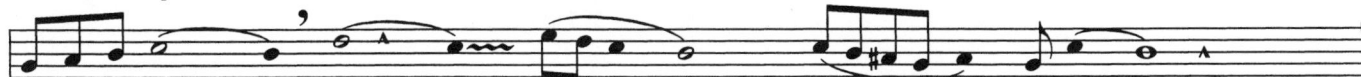

Hakimi   Mukhalef

ah

(ya   babadunya)   'eyuni

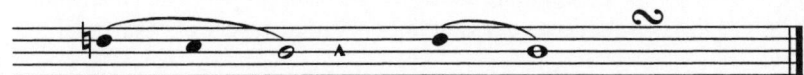

7

The Nawa Family

Although Sha'oubi files Nawa with the Nahawand family of maqams (1982, 14), some theorists prefer to think of things the other way around. Nawa is considered, at least alternately, to be a basic maqam, whereas Mohammed Qubanchi imported Nahawand to the Iraqi tradition (Bilal in Warkov 1987, 72). H. Rijab (1983, 171n1) regards Nawa as the parent maqam because it is found in thirteenth-century sources, whereas Nahawand is first mentioned a century later. At any rate, the family of maqams based on this lower tetrachord is small indeed: aside from Nawa and Nahawand, only Khanabat remains. In terms of transposition, Nawa and Khanabat are based on G, Nahawand on G or C. Nahawand's melodic progression is a descent similar to Nawa, but is slightly wider by prominently featuring 5, and also differs in using a ♭7. Khanabat is clearly differentiated from both Nawa and Nahawand by its register, and a characteristic 4-1 gesture, and its integral compound lower Beyat tetrachord.

Nawa

Maqam Nawa uses the tahrir vocable *Aman* and is set to classical Arabic poetry accompanied by the iqa' Samah; the iqa' changes to Wahda during the first meyana, after which it returns to Samah for the rest of the maqam. The scale of Iraqi Nawa presented by B. Rijab (1985, 84) and apparent in Yusuf Omar's recording corresponds to Persian Nawa, differing from the Turkish-Mashreqi cognate Neva/Nawa (although there are some affinities with the fifth octave species of makam Neva). A curious idiosyncracy of Iraqi Nawa is the use of an F# leading tone in the instrumental refrain but not in the main vocal line; the refrain in iqa' Wahda (in the first meyana) also includes F#. Nawa presents the qit'a 'Ushaish instead of an independent tahrir at its beginning (cf., qit'a Jasas in maqam Segah), which accounts for the unique disjunct arc of its opening. 'Ushaish ends at the descent to D/5, the remaining portion (beginning on B♭) is in Nawa proper. The jalsa phrase leading to the qarar of the maqam, which appears before the two meyanas is essentially a varied repeat of 'Ushaish (i.e., the definitive 4-1 descent of Beyat, here transposed to 5).

Nawa is characterized by the juxtaposition of its regular fifth degree D♮ with a D♭ that functions as an upper-neighbor decoration of C. There are also brief appearances of C♭, alluding to Saba/1: at the conclusion of the first meyana, in sections ten and eleven, and in the teslim. The maqam is essentially strophic, featuring a series of short phrases (labelled "A" to "D" in the transcription) that recur in slightly variable combinations. Sha'oubi (1982, 92) describes what I have labelled phrases "A" and "D" as Ajam and Beyat respectively, creating the effect of a compound maqam. Yusuf Omar's delivery strings together short fragments separated by pauses throughout the maqam.

The iqa' changes to Wahda for the duration of the first meyana, designated as Mischin (H. Rijab 1983, 178; B. Rijab 1985, 88), which shifts the modal center to Beyat/5; the return to Nawa and iqa' Samah in Yusuf Omar's performance is rather abrupt. The instrumental interlude of the meyana features a descending line that also appears in the interlude of the meyana in maqam Hijaz Diwan. Section nine of Yusuf Omar's performance corresponds to the placement of qit'a Mo'at (Sha'oubi 1982, 92) or Sunbule (B. Rijab 1985, 89), which are subtle variations on Omar's apparent rendering of phrase "A." The second meyana in Husseini is usually followed by two short qit'as; while Arwah is clearly identifiable in Yusuf Omar's recording, it is difficult to distinguish between the end of Husseini and a separate 8-5 descent indicative of Juburi. The teslim repeats material that concluded the first meyana.

Other qit'as listed: Mahmudi, Nahawand, Sereng.
Qit'a I appearances in maqams: Nahawand, Taher.

Yusuf Omar performance:

Tahrir (Ush)	Nawa	Jls	Mey I/Mis	Mo'at	Nawa	Nawa	Ush	Mey II	Juburi	Arwah	Tes
1-5-6-1	5-7-5-1	5-5	5-8-1	4-3	5-1	5-1	1-5	7-5	8-5	5-3-7-5	7-1
	(♭5)		Bey/5 (♭8,♭6, ♮4)		(♭5)			Hus/1	Bey/5	Hus/1	♮4
Samah 36/4			Wahda 4/4	Samah 36/4							

Abbreviations: Bey=Beyat; Hus=Husseini; Jls=Jalsa; Mey=Meyana; Mis=Mischin; Tes=Teslim; Ush='Ushaish

Nawa

Yusuf Omar

(Inedit W. 268006)

4. Nawa (4:24)

a li lai

5. Nawa (6:04)

6. Nawa (7:33)   Jalsa

7. Meyana I/Mischin, iqa' changes to Wahda (8:15)

allakh

interlude (joze part, Segah)   Saba (8:50)

8. Meyana continued (9:14)

yaba yaba   ya

(9:54) link returning to iqa' Samah   refrain   (etc.)

9. Mo'at? (10:14)   10. Nawa (11:12)

11. Nawa (12:18)

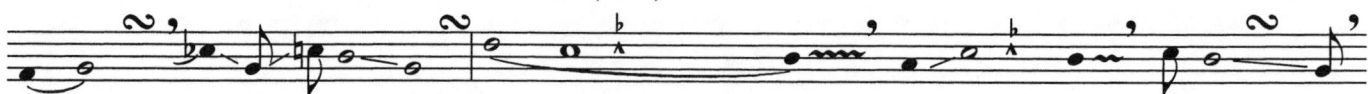

('Ushaish)

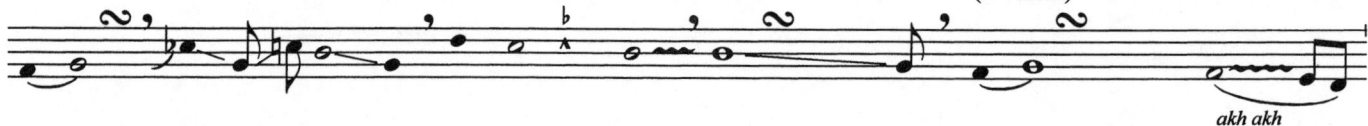

akh akh

Meyana II in Husseini (13:29)   Juburi?

Arwah

ya   ya

Teslim (14:30)

ya ba   ya   ya

hobi habib

Khanabat

Khanabat is set to classical Arabic, accompanied by the iqa' Yugrug. Sha'oubi uses the tahrir alfaz *Ah*; Hamid al-Saadi *Yar, aghayeman, oh yahabib*. While the main modality of Khanabat is in Nahawand, its tetrachord below 1 featured in the tahrir and teslim is Beyat/5, a "deceptive" cadential shift that produces the effect of a compound maqam. For this reason H. Rijab (1983, 175) considers Khanabat to be a member of the Beyat family. The melody of Khanabat itself frequently segues to melodic features of Nahawand throughout the rendition of this maqam by Sha'oubi. The main theme of Khanabat (4-2-4-1, emphasizing 2 and ending with a turn on 1) is reminiscent of the Persian gushehs Suz-o-Godaz and Bayat-e Raje.

Other qit'as listed: Bakhtiari, Mansuri.
Qit'a I appearances in maqams: Bheirzawi, Ibrahimi.

Sha'oubi Ibrahim performance:

Tahrir	Nahawand	Khan	Sayha I	Khan	Sayha II	Yatimi	Khan	Awshar	Dasht Arab/Teslim
1-5-4-1	4-1	4-1	5-1	4-1	5-1	4-1	4-1	2-6	5-2-5
Beyat/5								Segah/6	Beyat/5
Yugrug 12/4									

Abbreviations: Khan=Khanabat

Khanabat

Sha'oubi Ibrahim
(1982)

Nahawand

Imported and arranged by Mohammed Qubanchi, Nahawand can be set to either zheiri or classical poetry and has no rhythmic accompaniment or meyana, although the shift of range in qit'a Beyat produces the effect of one. Sha'oubi employs the tahrir alfaz *Ah, yaba*; Hamid al-Saadi *Aman, yaba*. Sha'oubi derives the scale for Nahawand as two conjunct Nahawand tetrachords C-F/F-B♭ (1982, 75). The idiomatic appearance of B♮ is due to melodic considerations (frequently raised ascending/lowered descending). The joze refrain in Sha'oubi (which is almost identical to his refrain in maqam Dasht) and his third section polarize 3, thereby evoking Ajam. The melody of qit'a Nawa is phrase "A" of maqam Nawa; the material from section 3 is reused as the teslim. While B. Rijab's description of Yatimi includes a variable ♭/♮2 (1985, 32), Sha'oubi's rendition remains natural.

Other qit'as listed: 'Araibun Ajam, Mthalatha.
Qit'a I appearances in maqams: Huizawi, Madmi, Nawa.

Sha'oubi Ibrahim performance:

Tahrir	Nahawand	Beyat	Nawa	Ajam	Beyat	Teslim
5-1	5-1	8-5-1	3-5-1	3-5-7-3	8-5	5-1
		Beyat/5			Beyat/5	

Nahawand

Sha'oubi Ibrahim
(1982)

1. Tahrir

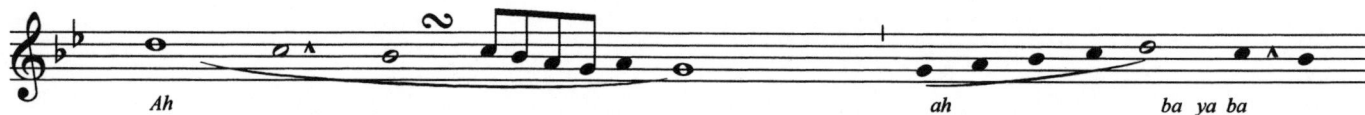

Ah   ah   ba ya ba

(joze refrain)

2. Nahawand

3. Nahawand   4. Beyat

5. Nawa

6. Ajam

7. Beyat (3x)   8. Nahawand/Teslim

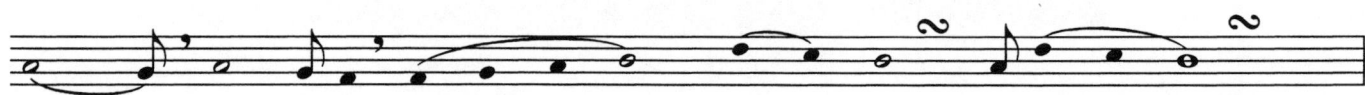

yaba

8

The Ajam/Jahargah Family

Although Jarhargah and Ajam are alternately considered to be basic maqams, B. Rijab (1985, 109) maintains that there is no Baghdadi version of Jahargah, and Scheherazade Hassan chose Ajam to represent the family in the Yusuf Omar recordings (1995a). On the other hand, with the exception of Ajam, all family members are in the naghmah of Jahargah. The family is characterized by differences in melodic themes, a proclivity for modulating to Saba/6, and range: Rashdi includes the tetrachord below the tonic, Jahargah functions within 1-5, Tahrir features an 8-5 descent, while Ajam covers a comparatively wide range above and below 1.

Ajam

Ajam is set to classical Arabic poetry and is performed without rhythmic accompaniment; its structure is quite straightforward. Sha'oubi employs the tahrir alfaz *Akh;* Hamid al-Saadi *Feryademan, janajan, yayar amirem wa.* The word Ajam denotes "foreign" or, more specifically, Persian. Without necessarily suggesting an historical connection, the melodic features of Ajam bear a fair resemblence to the Persian daramad of Mahur. Along with the same scale they share: an emphasis of 3 and 2 as recitation tones, a focus on the tetrachord below the tonic, a descending arc contour, and (in the Sha'oubi rendition) 6-7-1 cadences. Yusuf Omar cadences on 3 in one instance (section 4). The jalsa and teslim steer the melody down to the qarar (1), hence the full name of the maqam: Ajam 'Usheiran.

Other qit'as listed: Jahargah, 'Ushaish.
Qit'a I appearances in maqams: Beyat, Mischin, Nahawand, Nawa.

Yusuf Omar performance:

Tahrir	Ajam strophe	Jalsa	Meyana	Saba	Ajam	Teslim
1-5-4-1	1-4-5-1; 1-5-6-3; 3-5-5-1	1-1	3-6-2; 5-6	3-5-6	1-5-3	6-1
			Beyat/3; Beyat/6	Saba/6		

Ajam

Yusuf Omar
(Inedit W. 260063)

1. Tahrir (1:07)

Farya   de   man   janejan   a   man

ah   wei   lin   wa

2. Ajam (1:57)

3. Ajam (3:05)

4. Ajam (4:01)

5. (4:46)

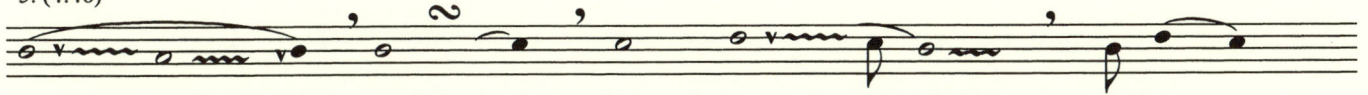

6. (5:47)

7. Ajam (6:59)

Jalsa (7:12)

akha   *a da*   *ya*

8. Meyana (7:58)

naza li liman   *ja*   *ah*

ah   *ha*

ja   nam   ah

9. Saba (9:04)

u   mi   dem

10. Saba (9:43)

Ajam (10:05)

Teslim

Jahargah

Other than Hamid al-Saadi's recording (EM CD 001), Sha'oubi is the only commercially available recording of maqam Jahargah, which appears to be somewhat rare in the repertoire. It is sung in classical Arabic, uses the tahrir alfaz *Ya, mahbub*, and is accompanied throughout by iqa' Yugrug; there is no meyana. The tahrir and theme of Jahargah focus on the lower tetrachord descending from 4 or 3, briefly touching 7 at the end of phrases. The upper tetrachord (though appearing in Jahargah below the tonic) is reserved for the type I qit'as Taher and Rashdi (both Jahargah family maqams), and the short jalsa before Saba.

Other qit'as listed: Abu Ata, Mahuri.
Qit'a I appearances in maqams: Ajam, Arwah, Bheirzawi, Mahmudi, Mukhalef, Saba, Taher.

Sha'oubi Ibrahim performance:

Tahrir	Jahargah	Jahargah	Jalsa	Jahargah	Saba	Saba	Taher	Rashdi	Jahargah	Teslim
1-3-1	4-6-1	4-1	3-5-1	3-5-1	1-6	1-3-6	1-5	1-2-5	4-1	4-5-1

Saba/6

Yugrug 12/4

Jahargah

Sha'oubi Ibrahim
(1982)

4. Jahargah

Saba

5. Saba

6. Taher

a wela   ba

7. Rashdi

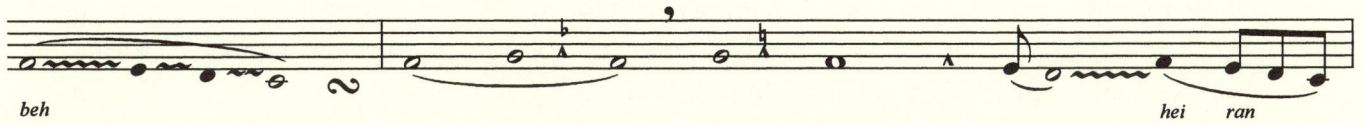

beh   *hei   ran*

8. Jahargah

Teslim

ya   ya

ya   *mah   bub*

Rashdi

Rashdi is set to zheiri poetry and iqa' Jurjina; there is no meyana. Sha'oubi uses the tahrir vocable *Awa*; Hamid al-Saadi *Ababyla aylem*. The melodic profile of Rashdi is similar to that of Jahargah, with a characteristic 4-2 motive. Its cadential phrase, however, emphasizes $\underline{6}$ and ends with $\underline{5}$, thereby briefly resembling the modal parallel of the Persian gushehs Ruh ol-Arwah and Dogah in Bayat-e Tork. Qit'a Aidin functions as both jalsa and teslim (cf., qit'a 'Ushaish in maqams Nawa, Arwah, and Sharqi Dogah), descending further to the qarar on $\underline{1}$.

Other qit'a listing: Taher.
Qit'a I appearance in maqam: Jahargah.

Sha'oubi Ibrahim performance:

Tahrir	Rashdi	Aidin	Rashdi	Khalili	Sharqi Rast	Rashdi	Saba	jins Jahargah	Teslim
1-4-$\underline{5}$	4-1-$\underline{6}$	$\underline{6}$-$\underline{1}$	4-$\underline{6}$	4-5-1	4-1	4-1	1-$\underline{6}$	3-4-$\underline{1}$	$\underline{1}$-$\underline{4}$-$\underline{1}$
							Saba/$\underline{6}$		

Jurjina 10/16

Rashdi

Sha'oubi Ibrahim
(1982)

Refrain "vamp"

1. Tahrir

Ah

2. Rashdi

Aidin

3. Rashdi

Khalili

Sharqi Rast   **4. Rashdi**

ya   *li   ya   ba   ya*   *gha nim*

Saba (repeat 3x)   **(return to Jahargah)**

(melody in iqa')

Teslim

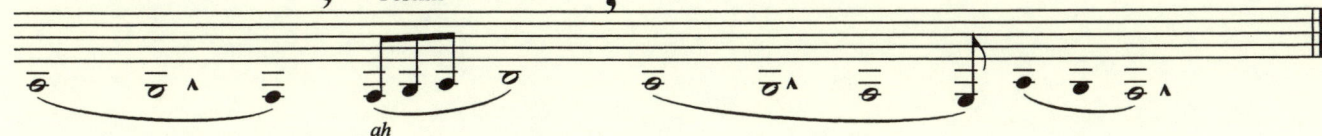

ah

Taher

Taher is set to classical Arabic poetry and iqa' Yugrug. Sha'oubi employs the tahrir vocables *Ya lalia, ya wela babeh*; Warkov (1987, 65n17) and Hamid al-Saadi give the Hebrew *Allelujah*. As performed by Sha'oubi, the qit'as Khalili and Sharqi Rast resemble
the character of the immediately following sections of Jahargah and Husseini; this particular juxtaposition illustrates the very subtle nature of modal differentiation within the
repertoire. Material from Aidin functions as the beginning of the teslim.

Other qit'as listed: Arwah, Mahuri, Mo'at al-Nawa, Nawa, Saba, Zanganai.
Qit'a I appearances in maqams: Arwah, Ibrahimi, Rashdi, Sharqi Rast.

Sha'oubi Ibrahim performance:

Tahrir	Taher	Taher	Aidin	S Mah	Taher	Juburi	Khalili	Sh R	Jhg	Husseini	Taher	Taher	Teslim
8-2'-5	8-2'-5	8-2'-6	6-1	2'	8-2'-5	2'-5	8-2'-6	6-8-5	3'-8	8-5-2'-6	5-8-5	8-6	6-7-1
				Bey/6		Bey/6		Rast/5		Hus/2			

Yugrug 12/4

Abbreviations: Bey=Beyat; Hus=Husseini; Jhg=Jahargah; S Mah=Sayha Mahmudi;
Sh R=Sharqi Rast

Taher

Sha'oubi Ibrahim
(1982)

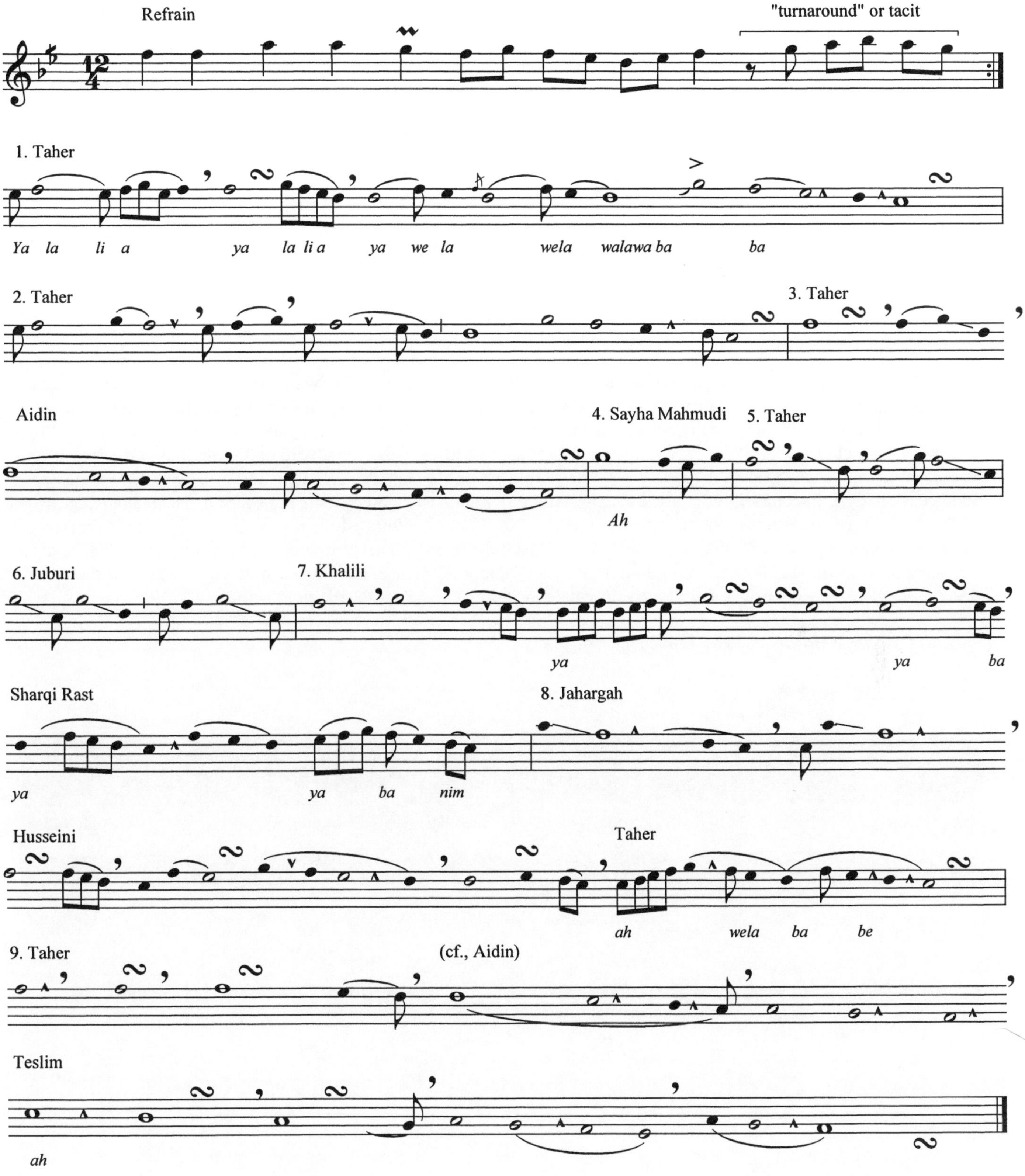

9

Miscellaneous Maqams

While maqam families are a useful and traditional means of categorizing repertoire, some maqams lie outside their purview.

Hleilawi

Hleilawi is set to zheiri poetry, accompanied by iqa' Jurjina, and employs the bedwa/tahrir alfaz *Weila*. Sha'oubi's tahrir is extremely brief and proceeds directly to the first line of poetry. The melody of Hleilawi itself features a compound structure: while remaining largely in Segah (in the upper octave), it can cadence in naghmah Rast (on 6), as in qit'a Sisani. The maqam concludes with a "deceptive" compound ending in a lower Hijaz tetrachord on G (Sha'oubi also descends just after the midpoint of the maqam in section six). The refrain alludes to naghmah Hozzam. The quality of 4 is variously ♭, ♮, and occasionally ♭. In contrast to the usual singing in free rhythm, some components are set to the accompanying Jurjina; while Sha'oubi provides transcriptions of these (1982, 100), I have transcribed them as performed. Yusuf Omar devotes more attention to a strophic B♭-G gesture (included in Sha'oubi as qit'a Qatar), excludes qit'a Mukhalef Kirkuk, and does not descend to the lower Hijaz tetrachord until the end of the performance. His intense performance creates the effect of one massively extended meyana. I arbitrarily designate the upper E♭ as 1 for the diagram below.

Other qit'as listed: Homayun, Nari, Mthalatha, Tiflis.

Sha'oubi Ibrahim performance:

Tahrir	Hle	Sis	Hle	Hozzam	Qatar	Hle	Hle	Desc	Hle	Segah	M Krk	Hle	Teslim
2-3	2-3	3-4-6	3-1	1-4-3	5-2	1-4-6	3-7	7-3	3-1	1-4-1	2-4-1	4-1	4-6; 6-3-3
					(♭5)			Hjz/3			(♭5)		Hjz/3
Jurjina 10/16													

Abbreviations: Desc=descent; Hjz=Hijaz; Hle=Hleilawi; M Krk=Mukhalef Kirkuk; Sis= Sisani; Tes=Teslim

Hleilawi

Sha'oubi Ibrahim

(1982)

Refrain

1. Tahrir   Hleilawi   Sisani

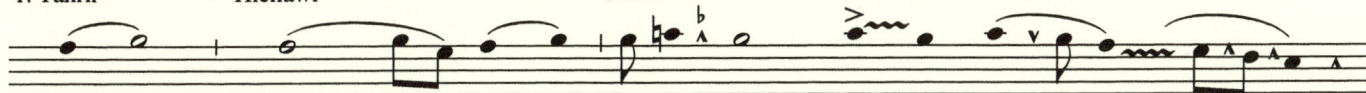

Wela   wela

2. Hleilawi

3. Hozzam (in iqa')

4. Qatar   5. Hleilawi   (naghmah Rast)

Ah

6. Hleilawi   descent

7. Hleilawi   8. Segah

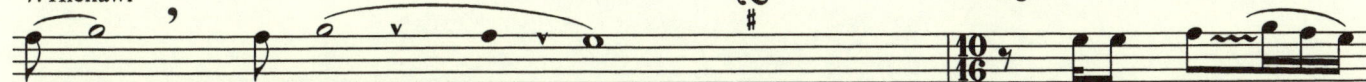

a wel   a

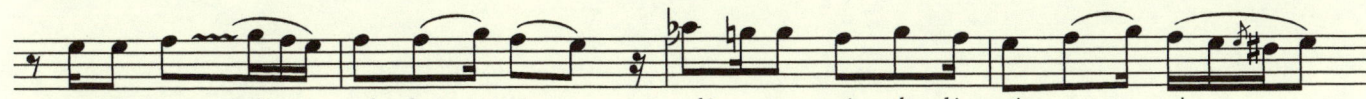

ya lil 'a   gil   de lu   ni   shi   nu si da bi tin su   ni

9. Mukhalef Kirkuk   10. Hleilawi   Teslim

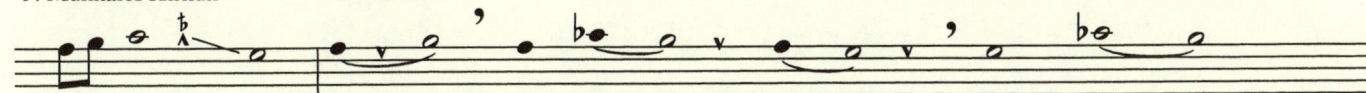

a ya ya   *kheyi*

kheyi   *ah*

weila   wel

Kurd

Imported and adapted by Mohammed Qubanchi (his 1928 recording of the maqam is available at www.iraqimusic.com), Kurd's independent status with regard to maqam family affiliation carries a strong political resonance (a similar independence is accorded to the Persian avaz Bayat-e Kord in the radifs of Nur Ali Boroumand and Abdollah Davami). Kurd is set to zheiri poetry without rhythmic accompaniment; its tahrir alfaz are *Leilia ya leil*; there is no meyana. The scale of Kurd is identical with its Mashreqi and Turkish cognates, here set on D. It also has a descending progression with the unusually wide range of a tenth. The jalsa phrase of Kurd is identical with that of Hijaz Kar (another Qubanchi composition featuring a wide range and descending progression). Kurd is a strophic maqam that includes a compound alternation with Beyat on 8.

Sha'oubi Ibrahim performance:

		(compound strophe)	
Tahrir	Kurd	Beyat	Kurd
8-3'-1	3'-1; 1-8-1	4'-5	8-5; 4-1-8-1
		Beyat/1	

Kurd

Sha'oubi Ibrahim
(1982)

1. Tahrir

Leil ... *lia   lei   lia   ya*

2. Kurd

leil

Ah ... *ya   ba*

3. Beyat (strophic phrase)

(return to Kurd)

Ah

4, 5, 6. Beyat/Kurd strophe

Mukhalef

The modal structure of Mukhalef is unique to the Iraqi tradition; while there is no correspondence with the Persian gusheh of the same name, it bears some resemblence to the gusheh Muye of Chahargah, the only structure that comes close to being a cognate in neighboring traditions. Mukhalef is set to zheiri poetry accompanied continuously by iqa' Yugrug; the tahrir alfaz are *Ah, kheyi, la wala 'eyuni*. Sources present a wide variety of scalar definitions of Mukhalef, the naghmah of which is usually restricted to a pentachord. Chabrier defines it as a hybrid of Segah and Saba (liner notes to EMI Pathe 2C 0666-95160). Although Mukhalef can be readily understood as a variant of Segah with a ♭3 (indeed, H. Rijab refers to it as *Segah al-a'raj*, "limping" or "crippled" Segah [1983, 154]), Chabrier's representation contains an anomalous G♮, lacks the B♭ found in other versions, and seems to force an awkward Mashreqi conception of the mode. The fourth degree of Mukhalef is given in sources as variously flat or kar bimol but some performances include its natural (e.g., Munir and Jamil Bashir) and an ornamental double-flat (Qubanchi, transcribed below); its kar bimol version seems the most common in performances. In performances 5 is usually flat but occasionally double-flat. The illustration of an octatonic pentachord in Sha'oubi (1982, 76) is somewhat difficult to reconcile with recorded sources: the E♮ is undoubtedly a misprint of E♭, resulting in a structure corroborated by Amiri (1990, 103). The pentachord in B. Rijab (1985, 21) presents the unusual interval G♭–A♭ between 3 and 4.

Mukhalef descends 4-1 and includes a definitive 3-1 cadential gesture (used somewhat like the core motif of Persian Shur) which is also tagged on to the endings of qit'as. The central section of qit'as (Kuyani, Sayha Mahmudi, 'Udhdhal, and Gulguli) of Sha'oubi's performance consists of 4-1 descents that are only differentiated by fine subtleties and textual content. Qit'a Jahargah (on 3) is included—interestingly the intervals are commutated to remain within the scale of Mukhalef (one would expect here an F♭ to function as 7 of Jahargah). The ear can be easily fooled with the melodic subtleties of Mukhalef and is drawn to take 3 or 4 as the tonal center of the maqam, whereby the eventual endings on 1 sound like "deceptive cadences."

Identifying qit'as in Qubanchi's performance, which seems largely strophic, is difficult; he includes Kuyani and Sayha Mahmudi but omits the clearly identifiable qit'as Mukhalef Kirkuk and 'Udhdhal (the latter can be identified through the alfaz *leil*). He sings similar but unidentified material at 4:14 (sung to the alfaz *yaba*) and 10:05 (*lesh yaba*). The instrumental accompaniment features a variety of refrains in a complex and thick heterophony that contributes to the ethereal quality to this performance. This transcription clearly illustrates the limitations and inadequacy of notating Iraqi maqam in detail, particularly Qubanchi's complex style. The symbol B♭♭ denotes a three-quarter tone above A♭.

Other qit'as listed: Aboush, Qatuli, Quriyat, Sereng/Mthalatha (and many others in al-Wardi 1969, 44)
Qit'a I appearances in maqams: Arwah, Awj, Awshar, Hakimi, Hijaz Kar, Mansuri, Nari, Orfa, Segah, Sharqi Rast/Esfahan.

Sha'oubi Ibrahim performance:

Tahrir	Mkh	Mkh	M Krk	S Mah	Mkh	Kyn	Jhg	Udh	Mkh	Gulguli	Teslim
2-1-3-1-4-1	4 /5-1	4 /5-1	4-1	4-5-1	5-3	4-1	3-1	4-5-1	4 /5-1	4-5-1	2-7-1
			(♭♭5)			(♭♭5)		(♭♭5)			

Yugrug 12/4

Abbreviations: Jhg=Jahargah; Kyn=Kuyani; Mkh=Mukhalef; M Krk=Mukhalef Kirkuk; S Mah=Sayha Mahmudi; Udh='Udhdhal

Mukhalef

Various definitions of naghmah Mukhalef

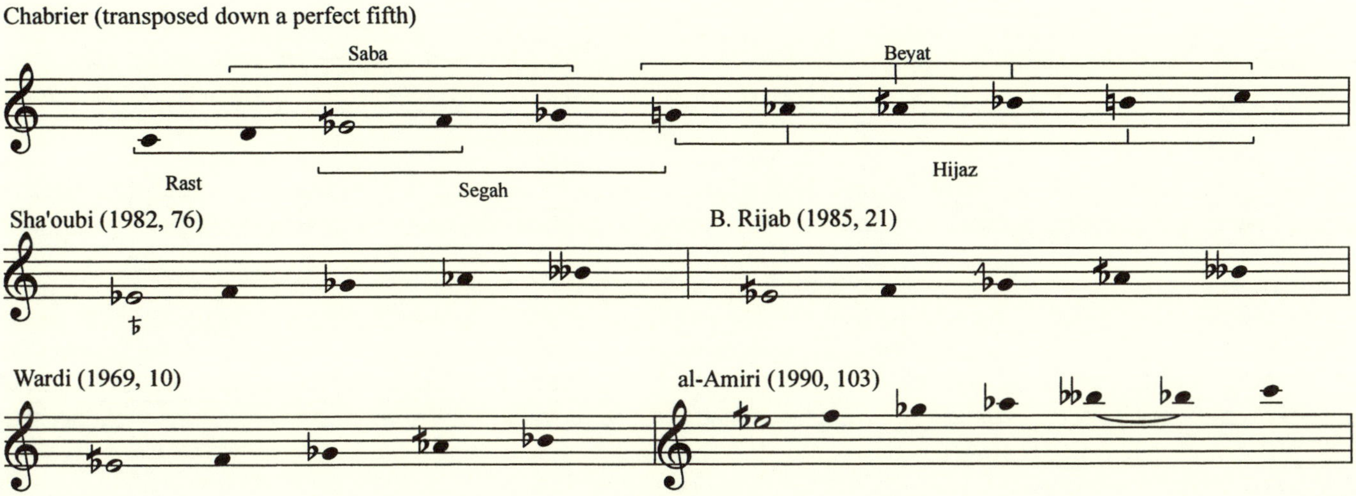

Sha'oubi Ibrahim
(1982)

Mukhalef Kirkuk

a   ya   ya

5. Sayha Mahmudi

ah   ah

6. Mukhalef   Kuyani

ya   ba   ya   yab   ya yab

7. Jahargah

'Udhdhal

liel   li   el   li   el   le   el   leluya

8. Mukhalef

9. Gulguli

10. Gulguli

Teslim

kheyi   a   'e   yu   ni

Mukhalef

Mohammed Qubanchi
(AAA 097)

Introduction (joze part)

1. Tahrir (0:25)

Ah

kheyi

2. Mukhalef (1:03)

la   wa   la   la   wa   la   la   wal   wa ya   yu   ni

la   wa   lah   la   wa   la lah   wa   la lah   wa la ya   yu

ni   ha

3. Mukhalef (2:02)

ma   li   a   ral ham   ma li   a ral ham   wib cha fi   mi gi dho shad   ma   li   a ralham wib cha   fi   mi gi

dho   shad   a   wimnil wilif   ad   wim nil wi li   fad   man   a   li u mu   shad

4. Mukhalef (3:22)

ya am mi wi ni wilif ad   man a li u muru shad   ah

5. Mukhalef (3:57)

ah   kh majnun ga lau majnun ga lau a la mak

qit'a? (4:14)

tul   a la   mak a la mak tul umrak shat ya   ba   ya ba

ya ba   ya ba   ya ba ya   ba ya ba ya   a ba i ya wa wa wa wa ha

6. Sayha Mahmudi (5:13)

ah   min jur din ya i ra   si mi nil ma da mi su fa

waw wa haw   akh

7. Mukhalef (6:02)

min jur din yai ra   si   ras i   min il mi dam i

ah   kh   ra si mi nil mi dam mi su fa

ya   la i mi kuf fi la mak   ya la i mi   ya la i mi ku fi la mak ku fi la mak u shuf u shuf is su fat

8. Mukhalef (7:18) **Kuyani (7:25)**

kh ya lai mi ku fi la mak u shu (?) fat ya bi a ya bia ya bia ya bi yab

ya yab ya yab yaya ye a ba

9. Mukhalef (8:04)

la hi ji min de re tin e shi bi he e shi bi he ma suf

(Jahargah?)

fa ah akh

10. 'Udhdhal (9:05)

la li be he na ga tin tir a wa la li shat wa la li shat

de ye ya ya ya ya ya i a i di ye ya ya ye ya yai de ye ya ya i

i ya i ya ya huh huh ha mua

11. Mukhalef (Gulguli?) (9:47)

ya ba lesh am mi lesh u yo ni lesh lesh kaz ri ha

wa   ku ri ya   de man   il li eh   di de   ya man il lesh

lesh   lesh   ba

ya ba   ya ba   ya ba   a ba

12. Mukhalef (Gulguli?) (10:34)

a   ni   min en   win tam   nein   hal   bal wam nein   ta   yih   tayih   o   gha rib

gharib   gharib   di dal uni   (??)

Glossary

alfaz: vocables or short textual phrases (in Arabic, Turkish, Persian, occasionally Kurdish and Hebrew) that are prescribed to specific components of a maqam.

asliyah: a basic maqam from which others are derived.

bedwa: synonymous with tahrir but considered to be shorter and/or in a high register.

chalghi: 1) the traditional ensemble for accompanying Iraqi maqam consisting of santur, joze, riqq, and darabouka; 2) traditional all-night social gatherings in private homes that include food, drink, dance, rest, and maqam performance.

dastgah: traditional modal category or subset of modes in Persian art music.

dulab: a short, introductory, metrical, instrumental prelude or interlude.

gusheh: an individual mode assigned a specific melody in Persian classical music.

iqa': a rhythmic mode.

jalsa: a cadential formula that marks a formal division in an Iraqi maqam.

jins: tetrachord.

joze: a spike fiddle used in Iraqi art music.

kar bimol: a note or interval flattened by a "quarter-tone" (the less common *kar diyes* refers to a "quarter-tone" sharp).

Mashreqi: the Eastern Mediterranean countries of the Arab world.

meyana: the climax of a maqam featuring alfaz and melismata in a high register.

moqadamme: a short, metrical instrumental composition that begins the performance of an Iraqi maqam.

muhasiba: improvised instrumental responses between sections of singing.

naghmah: Iraqi term for scale of a maqam.

pesta: a composed, light, metrical song that concludes a maqam performance.

qarar: lowest pitch of a maqam.

qit'a: submode with a prescribed melody which may be the transposition of the tahrir or main theme of another maqam (type I qit'a) or an entirely separate collection of melodies (type II).

radif: the modal repertoire of Persian art music consisting of gushehs organized into collections (dastgahs or avazes).

tahrir: introductory vocal component of an Iraqi maqam with a prescribed melody and alfaz.

teslim: final, cadential component of an Iraqi maqam before the pesta.

zheiri: poetry in colloquial Iraqi Arabic used in some Iraqi maqams.

Bibliography

Abu-Haidar, Farida. "The Poetic Content of the Iraqi Maqam." *Journal of Arabic Literature* 19, no. 2 (1988): 128–41.

Al-Amiri, Thamir Abdul Hassan. *Al-Maqam al-'Iraqi.* Baghdad: Dar al shu'un al-thakafiyya, Wizarat al-thakafa wal I'lam, 1990.

Al-Basri, Hamid. "Alhijaz sort (*sic*) in Iraki Makam." *Musica oral del sur: Revista internacional* 2 (1996): 207–15.

Bilal, 'Abd al-Wahhab. "Al-Maqamat al-Iraqiyah." *'Alam al-Fikr* 1 (1975): 33–102.

Bor, Joep. *The Raga Guide.* London: Nimbus Records, 1999.

Bradley, Hank. *Counterfeiting, Stealing and Cultural Plundering: A Manual of Applied Ethnomusicology.* Seattle: Mill Gulch Music, 1989.

Chabrier, Jean-Claude. "Analyse d'une 'improvisation' en mode Farahfaza." In *L'Improvisation dans les musiques des traditions orale,* edited by Bernard Lortat-Jacob, 159–76. Paris: SELAF, 1987.

During, Jean. *La musique iranienne: Tradition et evolution.* Paris: Editions Recherche sur la civilisation, 1984.

———. "Théories et practiques de la gamme iranienne." *Revue de Musicologie* 71, no. 1–2 (1985): 7–118.

———. *La musique traditionelle de l'Azerbayjan et la science des mugams.* Baden-Baden: Koernen, 1988.

———. *Le Repertoire modele de la musique iranienne: Radif de tar et setar de Mirza Abdollah, Version de Nur Ali Boroumand.* Tehran: Soroush, 1991.

———. "Tradition and History: The Case of Iran." In *The Garland Encyclopedia of World Music, vol. 6: The Middle East* edited by Virginia Danielson, et al., 853–64. New York: Garland, 2002.

Elsner, Jürgen. "Der irakische Maqam." In *Oriental Musik,* edited by Jürgen Elsner & Gisa Jähnichen, 131–83. Berlin: Humboldt University, 1992.

———. "Listening to Arabic Music." *World of Music* 39, no. 2 (1997): 111–26.

———. *Maqam, Raga, Zeilen melodik Konzeptionen und Prinzipien der Musikproduction: Arbeitstagung der Study group "maqam" beim ICTM vom 28. Juni bis 2. Juli 1988 in Berlin.* Berlin: ICTM, 1989.

Elsner, Jürgen and Gisa Jähnichen, eds. *Regionale Maqam: Traditionen in Geschichte und Gegenwart, Teil 1&II.* Berlin: ICTM, 1992.

d'Erlanger, Rudolph. *La Musique arabe, vol. 5.* Paris: Geunther, 1949.

Farhat, Hormoz. *The Dastgah Concept in Persian Classical Music.* Cambridge: University of Cambridge Press, 1991.

Feldman, Walter. *Music of the Ottoman Court: Makam, Composition and the early Ottoman Instrumental Repertoire.* Berlin: VWB Verlag fur Wissenschaft und Bildung, 1996.

Guenon, Rene. *Man and His Becoming According to the Vedanta.* London: Luzac, 1945.

Hassan, Scheherazade Qassim. "Le makam Irakien: Structures et realisations." In *L'Improvisation dans les musiques des traditions orale,* edited by Bernard Lortat-Jacob, 143–49. Paris: SELAF, 1987.

———. "Some Islamic non-Arabic elements of influence on the repertory of *al maqam al'iraqi* in Baghdad." In *Maqam, Raga, Zeilen melodik Konzeptionen und Prinzipien der Musikproduction: Arbeitstagung der Study group "maqam" beim ICTM vom 28. Juni bis 2. Juli 1988 in Berlin,* edited by Jürgen Elsner, 148–55. Berlin: ICTM, 1989.

———. "Choix de la musique et de la representation Irakiennes au Congres du Caire: vers un etude de contexts." In *Musique Arabe: Le Congres du Caire de 1932,* edited by Philippe Vigreux, 123–45. Cairo: CEDEJ, 1992.

————. "Survey of Written Sources on Iraqi Maqam." In *Regionale Maqam: Traditionen in Geschichte und Gegenwart, Teil 1,* edited by Jürgen Elsner and Gisa Jähnichen, 252–75. Berlin: ICTM, 1992a.

————. *Chants de Baghdad par l'ensemble al Tchalgi al-Baghdadi* CD notes, Institut du Monde Arabe CD-IMA 18, 1995.

————. *Iraqi Maqam—The Baghdad Tradition: A Tribute to Yusuf Omar (1918–1987)* CD notes, Inedit W.260063, 1995a.

————. "Iraqi Maqam: Transmission, Teaching and Learning." Unpublished paper read at the second meeting of the study group for the Music of the Arab World, University of Oxford, la maison française, October 1996.

————. *Maqams of Baghdad, Yusuf Omar* CD notes, Ocora OCR C.580066, 1996a.

————. "Iraq" In *New Grove Dictionary of Music, vol. 12,* edited by Stanley Sadie, 546–56. New York: Grove's Dictionaries, 2001.

————. "The Iraqi Maqam and Its Transmission." In *The Garland Encyclopedia of World Music, Vol. 6: The Middle East,* edited by Virginia Danielson, et al., 311–16. New York: Garland, 2002.

Jarrett, Keith. *The Köln Concert: For piano.* New York: Schott, 1991.

Kaufmann, Walter. *The Ragas of North India.* Bloomington, Ind.: University of Indiana Press.

Al-Khalil, Ibrahim Sha'oubi. *Dalil al-angham li tullab al-maqam.* Baghdad: Manshurat al markaz al-dawli li dirsat al-musiqa al-taklidiyya/Da'irat al-funun al-musiqa/Wizarat al-thakafia wal I'lam, 1982.

Kippen, James. "Wajid Revisited: A Reassessment of Robert Gottlieb's Tabla Study, and a New Transcription of the Solo of Wajid Hussain Khan of Lucknow." *Asian Music* 18, no. 2 (Spring/Summer 2002): 111–74.

Kojaman, Yeheskel. *Al-Musiqa al-fanniyag al-mu'asirah fi al-'Iraq.* London: Akt lil Tarajim al-'Arabiyya, 1978.

————. "The Jewish Role in Iraqi Music." *Dangoor.* http://www.dangoor.com/72page42.html (21 Dec. 2000).

————. *The Maqam Music Tradition of Iraq.* London: Y. Kojaman, 2000.

Marcus, Scott. "Arab Music Theory in the Modern Period." Ph.D. diss., University of California at Los Angeles, 1989.

————. "Modulation in Arab Music: Documenting oral concepts, performance rules and strategies." *Ethnomusicology* 36, no. 2 (Spring/Summer 1992): 171–95.

————. "The Eastern Arab System of Melodic Modes in Theory and Practice: A Case Study of *Maqam Bayyati.*" In *The Garland Encyclopedia of World Music, Vol. 6: The Middle East* edited by Virginia Danielson, et al., 33–44. New York: Garland, 2002.

Markoff, Irene. "Musical Theory, Performance, and the Contemporary Baglama Specialist." Ph.D. diss., University of Washington, 1986.

Moussali, Bernard. *Rashid al-Gundarji, The Falsetto of Baghdad* CD notes, Al Sur ALCD 183, 1996.

————. *Husayn al-Azami, Chants d'extase en Irak* CD notes, Al Sur ALCD 129, 1996a.

Nelson, David. "Mrdangam Mind: The Tani Avartanam in Karnatak Music." Ph.D. diss., Wesleyan University, Middletown, Conn., 1991.

Nettl, Bruno. *The Radif of Persian Music.* Champaign, Ill.: Elephant & Cat, 1992.

Ogger, Thomas. *Maqam Segah/Segah: Vergliech der Kunstmusik des irak und Iran anhand eines maqam Modells (Beitrage zur Ethnomusikologie, Bd. 15).* Hamburg: K. D. Wagner, 1987.

Powers, Harold. "Mode." In *New Groves Dictionary of Music and Musicians, Vol.12,* edited by Stanley Sadie, 377–450. London: MacMillan, 1980.

————. "International segah and its nominal equivalents in Central Asia and Kashmir." In *Maqam, Raga, Zeilen melodik Konzeptionen und Prinzipien der Musikproduction: Arbeitstagung der Study group "maqam" beim ICTM vom 28. Juni bis 2. Juli 1988 in Berlin,* edited by Jürgen Elsner, 40–85. Berlin: ICTM, 1989.

Qureshi, Regula Burckhardt. "Other Musicologies: Exploring issues and confronting practice in India." In *Rethinking Music,* edited by Nicholas Cook and Mark Everist, 311–35. Oxford: Oxford University Press, 2001.

Al-Rijab, Bahir. *Usul ghina' al-maqam al-Baghdadi.* Baghdad: Matba'at offset al-Rassam, 1985.

Al-Rijab, Mohamad Hashim (al Hajj). *Al-maqam al-'Iraqi.* (2nd ed.) Baghdad: Manshurat maktabat almuthanna, Matba'at al-Irshad, 1983 [1st ed. 1961].

Saleh, Mohammed. "L'organisation mélodique et rythmique des maqamat." Ph.D. diss., University of Paris IV-Sorbonne, 1985.

Sawa, George. *Musical Performance in the Early 'Abbasid era 132–320 A.H./750–932 A.D.* Toronto: Pontical Institute of Medieval Studies, 1989.

Small, Christopher. *Musicking: The Meanings of Performing and Listening.* Hanover: University Press of New England, 1998.

Signell, Karl. *Makam: Modal Practice in Turkish Art Music.* Seattle: Asian Music Press, 1977.

———. "Contemporary Turkish Makam Practice." In *The Garland Encyclopedia of World Music, vol. 6: The Middle East* edited by Virginia Danielson, et al., 47–58. New York: Garland, 2002.

Sorrell, Neil and Ram Narayan. *Indian Music in Performance: A Practical Introduction.* Manchester: University of Manchester Press, 1980.

Suchoff, Benjamin, ed. *Bela Bartok Essays.* London: Faber & Faber, 1976.

Tala'i, Dariush. *Traditional Persian Art Music: The Radif of Mirza Abdollah.* Costa Mesa, Calif.: Mazda, 2000.

Touma, Habib. *Der Maqam Beyati im arabischen Taqsim (Beitrage zur Ethnomusikologie, Bd. 3).* Hamburg: K. D. Wagner, 1976.

———. *The Music of the Arabs.* Portland, Ore.: Amadeus Press, 1996.

Tsuge, Gen'ichi. "A Note on the Iraqi Maqam." *Asian Music* 4, no. 1 (1972): 59–66.

———. "Iraq: 'ud classique arabe par Munir Bashir" record review, *Asian Music* 4, no. 2 (1972a): 36–37.

Van der Linden, Neil. "'Maqam Singing' in Modern Iraq." *Aramusic.* 1999. http://www.aramusic.com/maqam (Oct. 1999).

———. "The Classical Iraqi *Maqam* and Its Survival." In *Colors of Enchantment* edited by Sherifa Zuhur, 321–35. Cairo: The American University in Cairo Press, 2001.

Al-Wardi, Hamoudi. *Al-Maqamat al-'Iraqiya: Maqam al-Mukhalef.* Baghdad: Asad Press, 1969.

Warkov, Esther. "Revitalization of Iraqi-Jewish Instrumental Traditions of Israel: The Persistent Centrality of an Outsider Tradition." *Asian Music* 17, no. 2 (1986): 9–31.

———. "The Urban Arabic Repertoire of Jewish Professional Musicians in Iraq and Israel: Instrumental Improvisation and Culture Change." Ph.D. diss., Hebrew University (Jerusalem), 1987.

Wegner, Ulrich. *Abudiya und Muwwal: Untersuchen zur sprachlish-musikalishen Gestalung im südirakischen Volksgesang (Beitrage zur Ethnomusikologie, Bd. 12).* Hamburg: K. D. Wagner, 1982.

Widdess, Richard. "Involving the Performers in Transcription and Analysis: A Collaborative Approach to Dhrupad." *Ethnomusicology* 38, no. 1 (Winter 1994): 59–79.

Wilber, Ken. *A Theory of Everything.* Boston: Shambhala, 2000.

Zeranska-Kominek, Slawomira. "Mode: Process and/or Structure—An Analytical Study of the Turkmen Mukam Gökpede." In *Secondo Convegno Europeo di analise musicale,* edited by Rossana Dalmonte and Mario Baroni, 249–58. Trento: Università degli Studi di Trento, 1992.

———. "Some methodological points concerning the concept of maqam: A case study of the Turkmen mukam." In *Regionale Maqam: Traditionen in Geschichte und Gegenwart, Teil 2,* edited by Jürgen Elsner and Gisa Jähnichen, 510–23. Berlin: ICTM, 1992.

Zonis, Ella. *Classical Persian Music: An Introduction.* Cambridge: Harvard University Press, 1973.

Discography

al-A'dhami, Hussein. *Chants d'extase en Irak*. Al Sur, ALCD 129 [Beyat, Mukhalef].

———. *The Passion of the 1001 Nights and the Baghdad School of Song*. Al-Sur, ALCD 151 [Awj, Saba, Awshar, Homayun, Rast Panjgah].

———. *Chants de Baghdad,* Institut du Monde Arab CD IMA 18 [Homayun, Awj, Nahawand, Dasht, Panjgah].

———. *The Music of the Arabs*. Amadeus Press (disc published with Touma 1996) [Urfa].

Ali, Farida Mohammed. *Classical Music of Iraq*. Samarkand Records, Sam CD 9001.

———. *Mawal and Maqamat of Iraq*. Samarkand Records, Sam CD 9004.

Jrifani, Muhammad. *Iqa'at—Traditional Rhythmic Structures*. Auvidis D 8044 [Basrah tradition: Mukhalef].

Omar, Yusuf. *Modal Music and Improvisation, Vol.3—Arabian Music: Maqam*. Philips 658006 [Mansuri].

———. *Iraqi Maqam Baghdad Tradition—A Tribute to Yusuf Omar (1918–1987)*. Inedit W.260063 [Rast, Beyat, Nawa, Hijaz Diwan, Ajam, Mansuri].

———. *Iraq: The Maqams of Baghdad*. Ocora C.580066 [Husseini, Hleilawi, Segah].

Qubanchi, Mohammed. *Le Maqam en Irak—Congres du Caire, 1932. Vols 1 & 2*. Les Artistes Arabes Associes/Club du disque Arabe. AAA-087 & 097 [Vol 1: Rast, Ibrahimi; Vol.2: Sharqi Dogah, Mukhalef, Bheirzawi, Madmi].

Qundarchi, Rashid. *The Falsetto of Baghdad*. Al Sur, ALCD 183 [Gulguli, Segah, Rast Turki, Saba, Mansuri, Nari, Mischin, Ibrahimi, Madmi].

al-Saadi, Hamid. *Al-Haneen*. EMEE EM CD 001 [Urfa, Saba, Jahargah].

———. *Al-Shawq*. EMEE EM CD 002 [Awshar, Hakimi, Rashdi].

———. *Al-Mahabba*. EMEE EM CD 003 [Panjgah, Hijaz Diwan, Sharqi Dogah].

———. *London Concert, Part One*. EMEE EM CD 004 [Panjgah, Rukbani].

———. *London Concert, Part Two*. EMEE EM CD 005 [Huizawi].

———. *Al-Wiqar*. EMEE EM CD 006 [Mansuri, Dasht, Nawa].

———. *Al-Huob Alluthri*. EMEE EM CD 007 [Beyat, Segah, Hijaz Kar].

———. *Al-Turath al-Khalid*. EMEE EM CD 008 [Jamal, Sa'idi Mubarqa, Hadidi, Ibrahimi].

Internet Sources

The following sites feature articles, mp3 files, and online CD sales of Iraqi maqam:

http://www.aramusic.com
http://www.iraqimusic.com
http://www.iraq4u.com

General Index

acquisition, 3, 5, 12

alfaz, 17, 18, 20, 23, 24–29, 42

Arabic language, 3, 4, 9, 17, 33, 42; Iraqi dialect, 7, 17, 42, 44. *See also* poetry

avaz, 17, 25, 62, 64, 87, 99, 124, 150, 178

Azerbaijan, musical tradition of, 2, 16, 17, 20

Baghdad, musical tradition of, 2, 4, 30, 34, 44, 45, 165

Bartok, Bela, 1, 8n1

Bashir, Jamil, 1, 44n7, 180

Bashir, Munir, 1, 33, 44n7, 180

bedwa, 18, 59, 126, 138, 176

cadences, 1, 6, 18, 20, 23, 64, 79, 92, 102; cadential formulae, 12; deceptive, 16, 176, 180. *See also* forud; teslim

Cantemir, Demetrius, 12

chalghi, 9, 17, 42

composition, 10, 12, 16, 18, 20, 42, 83, 178. *See also* maqam: importations to Iraq

compounding: processes, 16, 22, 23, 34, 43, 92, 104, 134, 156, 178; phrases in qit'as and maqams, 21, 34. *See also* fasl; form

dastgah, 18, 20, 21, 45n24, 45n25, 47, 76, 134

drones, 20–21, 64, 92

dulab, 18, 47, 52, 62, 104, 105, 129, 138

al-Farabi, 11

fasl, 42–43, 44

folk music, 3, 9n5, 33, 76, 102, 153

form, 2, 5, 6, 7, 16, 17, 18, 23, 33. *See also* strophes; repertoire, hierarchy

forud, 20, 44n6

gusheh, 20, 21, 30, 45n25, 47, 64, 99, 104, 111, 117, 124, 134, 153, 161, 172, 180

Hebrew language, 4, 17, 174

improvisation, 2, 5, 10, 17, 18, 21, 35, 44n6, 44n8, 104

India, musical tradition of, 1, 3, 10, 11, 12, 16, 30, 44n3, 44n4

interludes, 2, 6, 16, 18, 23, 35, 40, 47, 57, 104, 108, 109, 110, 129, 130, 149, 156, 159

intontation, 4, 10, 11; "quarter tones," 11; theory and practice, 4, 11, 83, 117, 124, 147, 153

iqa', 9n6, 23, 35, 36, 42, 173, 177

Iran, musical tradition of, 1, 2, 3, 10, 11, 12, 16, 20, 21, 30, 44n6, 44n10, 45n25, 117

Iraq, 1, 2, 8, 17; Iraqi people, 1, 2, 4, 8

Iraqi maqam: basic maqams, 4, 20, 21, 22, 34, 35, 42, 44, 45n22, 45n25; components, 3, 4, 7, 16, 17, 18–29, 31–33, 35, 44; compound maqams, 111, 156, 161, 176; free/strict, 33, 153; Iraqi sources and theorists, 4, 5, 9, 18, 23; maqam families, 33, 34, 35, 43, 44, 45n23, 45n25, 127–28; reciters, 2, 3, 4, 5, 8n3, 9n6; relation to West Asian traditions, 2; research and sources, 3, 4; rhythmic maqams, 6, 7, 18, 35, 37–41, 42; role of women, 5; sacred maqam tradition, 2, 9, 42; structures and terminology, 17–44; typology, 33–34; Western scholarship, 1, 3. *See also* composition; compounding processes; naghmah

Israel, Iraqi maqam tradition, 1, 3, 4, 30, 33

jalsa, 18, 20, 23, 33

Jarrett, Keith, 5, 6

joze, 4, 164

Kirkuk, 2

Kurdish: language, 4, 17, 18; maqam, 124

Maghreb, musical tradition of, 10, 12

makam (Turkish), 9, 12, 16, 22, 35, 44n5, 147, 156

maqam: cognate maqams, 2, 10, 12, 34, 44n1; importations to Iraq, 30, 34, 76, 99, 117, 156, 163, 178; nomenclature, 10, 23, 138; root positions, 11; West Asian structures and characteristics, 10–17. *See also* compounding processes; modulation; naghmah; scale

al-Masaraf, 'Izzat, 30

Mashreq, musical tradition of, 10, 16, 22, 35, 64, 114, 180

melisma, 6, 16, 17, 18, 47, 89

melody, 5, 6, 7, 18, 21; melodic formulae, 10, 19, 20, 35, 37–40; melodic profile, 19, 24–29; melodic progression, 12, 16, 19, 21, 64, 79, 89, 92, 96, 102, 117, 124, 147, 156, 178

Mevlevi music, 11

meyana, 18, 20, 21, 23, 30, 31, 32, 33, 35

modes, 2, 4, 10; modal functions, 12–16; modal theory, 2, 3, 6, 9, 10–17, 92, 156; mode and mood, 10, 111, 147; rhythmic modes, 9, 35–36; tune-scale continuum, 10, 16, 20, 35. *See also* iqa'
modulation, 1, 2, 7, 11, 16, 17, 20, 21, 22, 23, 30, 43, 64, 76, 99, 111, 114, 117
moqadamme, 18
Mosul, 2
motives, 6, 12, 17, 21, 44, 62, 72, 73, 81, 92, 96, 99
musicians: Iraqi, 1, 6, 8, 33, 35, 42; Persian, 11; Syrian and Moroccan, 138

naghmah, 13–15, 21, 22, 23, 24, 25, 26, 28, 34, 43, 181
notation, 4, 5–7, 102

Omar, Yusuf, 2, 3, 4, 5, 6, 8–9, 18, 21, 23, 47, 48, 55, 64, 65, 69, 92, 93, 94, 104, 105, 106, 114, 129, 134, 138, 139, 140, 147, 153, 156, 157, 158, 165, 166, 176
ornamentation, 2, 4, 6, 7, 16, 17, 21, 35, 96, 102, 104, 132, 180; neighbor notes, 6, 7, 76, 102, 120, 124, 156
Ottoman music, 2

patriarchy, 5, 9n10
pedagogy, 4, 5, 10
performance practice, 2, 4, 5, 17, 18, 33
Persian language, 4, 17
pesta, 17, 18, 23, 35, 42, 87, 111
pitch: designation and nomenclature, 11; hierarchy, 12, 18; notation, 7
poetry, 2, 17, 18, 33, 42, 104, 120, 176; in classical Arabic, 47, 59, 64, 92, 96, 99, 102, 104, 111, 117, 120, 129, 134, 138, 147, 150, 156, 163, 165, 169, 174; zheiri, 17, 20, 35, 62, 73, 76, 79, 81, 83, 85, 87, 89, 111, 114, 122, 124, 132, 153, 161, 163, 172, 176, 178, 180. *See also* Arabic language

qarar, 18, 32, 59, 76, 147, 156, 165, 172
qit'as, 3, 4, 17, 18, 20–33, 35, 42, 44; distribution in repertoire, 21–22, 23, 24–29, 31–33; melodic profiles of, 24–29; rare or obsolete, 23; type I, 20, 21–22; type II, 20, 22–29, 42. *See also* submodes; specific listings in the "Index of Modes"
Qubanchi, Mohammed, 3, 5, 8–9, 30, 34, 47, 48, 49, 92, 114, 117, 122, 123, 124, 147, 156, 163, 178, 180, 183
Qundarchi, Rashid, 5, 30, 64, 65, 66, 122, 123, 134, 135, 183

radif, 10, 18, 21, 23, 34, 44n6, 45n24, 45n25, 139, 178
raga, 1, 10, 12, 16, 44n4
recordings, 1, 2, 3, 4, 5, 6, 7, 17, 23, 33, 35, 42, 44n7, 104, 114, 134, 147, 153, 165, 169, 178
refrain, in rhythmic maqams, 18, 23, 35, 37–41, 62, 73, 76, 89, 96, 111, 132, 156, 163, 176, 180, 181
repertoire (Iraqi), 1, 2, 3, 4, 5, 17, 18, 21, 22, 23, 30–35, 42–44, 47, 76, 99, 114, 126, 134; hierarchy, 30, 44; rare or obsolete, 21, 23, 30, 44n17, 91, 126, 139, 169, 174, 176

rhythm, 6, 7, 33, 111, 176; "free" or unmetered, 6, 10, 17, 176; rhythmic cycle, 6, 7, 35
Rijab, Bahir, 3, 4, 5, 6, 22, 23, 24, 27, 30, 44n14, 44n16, 92, 104, 129, 138, 139, 156, 163, 180, 181
Rijab, Hashim, 3, 4, 5, 8, 9, 18, 20, 21, 30, 33, 42, 43, 44n12, 47, 134, 150, 153, 156, 161, 165

al-Saadi, Hamid, 2, 3, 5, 7, 18, 20, 21, 23, 30, 33, 44n16, 44n19, 59, 83, 87, 89, 92, 99, 102, 104, 117, 122, 134, 147, 150, 153, 161, 163, 165, 169, 172, 174
sayha. *See* meyana
scales, 5, 7, 10, 11, 12, 13–15, 16, 17, 18, 21, 22, 23, 33, 34, 35, 42, 43; chromatic alterations and ascending-descending forms, 11, 12, 139, 147, 150, 163, 176; component tetrachords, 12, 13–15; octave species, 10, 11, 12, 13, 15, 16, 44. *See also* naghmah
Schenker, Heinrich, 6
Shaltagh, Rahmat Allah, 30
Sha'oubi Ibrahim (Ibrahim Sha'oubi al-Khalil), 4, 5, 6, 7, 9, 17, 19, 20, 21, 22, 23, 27, 30, 34, 35, 37, 40, 41, 44n19, 59, 60, 62, 63, 64, 73–91, 92, 96, 97, 99, 100, 102, 103, 104, 105, 111–25, 129–33, 134, 138, 139, 147–55, 156, 161–64, 165, 169–75, 176–79, 180, 181
solfege, 11
strophes, 2, 17, 18, 21, 23, 33, 87, 92, 93, 117, 124, 134, 150, 153, 156, 165, 176, 178, 180
style, 1, 2, 5, 12, 20, 42
submodes, 3, 16, 20, 22. *See also* Iraqi maqam, components; qit'as

tahrir, 17, 18, 19, 20, 21, 23, 33, 35, 42; profile of, 19
terminology, 12, 17
teslim, 17, 18, 20, 23, 33, 35, 42, 44
tetrachords (jins), 7, 10, 11, 12, 13–15, 20, 21, 23, 32, 35; root position of, 11
theory, 2, 4, 6, 10, 11, 12, 17, 23, 47, 156; and practice, 5, 6, 8, 11
transcription, 4, 5–7, 9, 23, 92, 124, 126, 129, 176, 180
transliteration, 7
transmission, 3, 4, 5, 42
transposition 2, 7, 11, 16, 17, 20, 21, 22, 23, 29, 35, 37–41, 64, 87, 96, 114, 134, 139, 156
Turkey, musical tradition of, 1, 9, 10, 11, 12, 16, 18, 21, 22, 23, 34, 35, 42, 83, 134, 147
Turkish language, 4, 17
Turkish-Mashreqi musical tradition, 1, 2, 12, 20, 21, 34, 59, 64, 92, 96, 134, 138, 156, 178

variation, 10, 11, 16, 17, 21, 35, 42, 126, 138, 139, 156; variants, 21, 73, 89, 92, 102, 104, 180
vocables, 2, 6, 17. *See also* alfaz
vocal style and technique, 17, 20, 180

Zaydan, Ahmad, 30, 44, 99
zheiri. *See* poetry, zheiri

Index of Modes

Aboush, 22, 23, 25, 31, 32, 33, 73, 74, 76, 78, 81, 85, 129, 130, 132, 133, 134, 138, 180
Abu Ata, 23, 31, 32, 44n17, 64, 87, 96, 99, 169
Aidin, 24, 81, 82, 83, 172, 173, 174, 175
Afshari, 21, 62, 150
Ajam, 11, 12, 13, 15, 18, 19, 20, 22, 31, 32, 33, 34, 43, 64, 65, 67, 71, 76, 83, 84, 129, 147, 156, 163, 164, 165–68, 169
'Araibun, 18, 31, 34, 37, 111–13
'Araibun Ajam, 21, 22, 30, 31, 32, 33, 34, 43, 76, 77, 85, 86, 91, 104, 111, 112, 120, 122, 123, 124, 125, 126, 127, 163
'Araibun Arab, 30, 31, 32, 34, 43, 44n11, 44n18, 64, 73, 81, 111, 112, 113, 126
'Ardhibar/'Alizabar, 21, 22, 25, 32, 42, 76, 78, 81
Arwah, 21, 22, 31, 32, 33, 34, 41, 43, 79, 89, 90, 92, 96–98, 99, 102, 103, 134, 137, 147, 156, 157, 160, 169, 172, 174, 180
Awj, 11, 19, 20, 21, 31, 32, 33, 34, 43, 45n22, 144, 147–49, 153, 180
Awshar, 20, 22, 31, 32, 33, 34, 129, 130, 138, 139, 150–52, 161, 162, 180

Bajalan, 21, 22, 30, 31, 33, 34, 35, 42, 43, 124, 139
Bakhtiar, 22, 26, 30, 32, 161
Bashiri, 21, 30, 33, 34
Bastenegar, 34, 44n15, 129, 138, 139
Bayat-e Kord, 30, 178
Bayat-e Raje, 111, 161
Bayat-e Tork, 124, 172
Beyat, 13, 14, 15, 16, 18, 19, 20, 21, 22, 23, 25, 30, 31, 32, 34, 35, 42, 43, 45n24, 47, 48, 50, 64–72, 73, 76, 77, 79, 80, 81, 87, 89, 91, 92, 93, 96, 99, 102, 105, 111, 113, 117, 119, 122, 124, 126, 129, 132, 134, 135, 138, 139, 141, 147, 156, 157, 161, 162, 163, 164, 165, 174, 178, 179
Beyat Ajam, 21, 30, 31, 34, 42, 126, 127
Bheirzawi, 22, 31, 32, 33, 34, 35, 38, 42, 44, 64, 73–75, 76, 78, 79, 81, 83, 85, 86, 111, 113, 122, 124, 161, 169
Bidad, 104, 117
Buselik, 11, 21, 22, 24, 31, 92, 93, 94, 104, 105, 110

Chahargah, 21, 134, 147, 153, 180

Dasht, 18, 19, 21, 22, 30, 31, 32, 33, 34, 43, 92, 98, 99–101, 102, 103, 120, 121, 161, 162, 163
Dashti, 20, 31, 32, 96, 99
Dogah, 172

Evc, 147

Gulguli, 21, 22, 30, 32, 33, 34, 180, 182, 185, 186

Hadidi, 31, 34, 35, 38, 43, 81, 85, 89, 122, 132–33, 134
Hakimi, 21, 22, 23, 31, 32, 33, 34, 35, 37, 43, 76, 85, 114, 115, 116, 138, 139, 143, 144, 147, 148, 153–55, 180
Hijaz, 11, 12, 13, 14, 15, 16, 22, 23, 35, 43, 44n2, 45n23, 48, 59, 60, 85, 96, 99, 104, 105, 109, 110, 111, 117, 122, 124, 126, 127, 132, 134, 138, 147, 153, 176
Hijaz Achough, 21, 22, 30, 31, 33, 34, 104, 105, 109, 126, 127
Hijaz Diwan, 20, 21, 22, 31, 32, 33, 34, 35, 40, 42, 43, 65, 76, 92, 99, 102, 104–10, 111, 117, 118, 126, 129, 134, 156
Hijaz Gharib, 22, 23, 25, 30, 31, 32, 96, 98, 99, 101, 117, 119, 120, 121, 122, 123, 126, 127, 134
Hijaz Kar, 14, 21, 22, 30, 31, 34, 35, 104, 114–16, 153, 178, 180
Hijaz Madani, 21, 22, 29, 31, 33, 47, 48, 58, 104, 105, 110
Hijaz Shaytani, 20, 21, 22, 30, 31, 33, 34, 35, 42, 43, 48, 50, 56, 104, 105, 126, 127
Hleilawi, 31, 33, 34, 35, 41, 43, 87, 117, 124, 176–77
Homayun, 21, 30, 31, 32, 33, 34, 65, 104, 117–19, 120, 124, 125, 176
Hozzam, 15, 26, 154, 177
Huizawi, 30, 31, 32, 33, 34, 99, 104, 117, 120–21, 122, 163
Husseini, 14, 15, 18, 19, 20, 21, 22, 23, 28, 31, 32, 33, 34, 35, 42, 43, 76, 79, 89, 92–95, 96, 99, 101, 102, 103, 104, 105, 106, 107, 110, 120, 129, 134, 136, 147, 156, 157, 160, 174, 175

Ibrahimi, 21, 22, 31, 32, 33, 34, 35, 38, 43, 48, 50, 56, 64, 73, 76–78, 79, 81, 83, 85, 87, 92, 111, 113, 124, 134, 161, 174
Iraq, 11, 15, 31, 34, 132, 133, 138, 147

Jahargah, 11, 15, 21, 22, 23, 28, 31, 32, 33, 34, 35, 37, 43, 48, 64, 73, 75, 76, 81, 82, 92, 93, 96, 129, 131, 153, 165, 169–71, 172, 174, 175, 180, 182, 185
Jamal, 21, 22, 30, 32, 33, 34, 117, 120, 126, 127, 138, 139, 145

194

Jasas, 22, 23, 26, 33, 138, 139, 140, 156
Juburi, 22, 23, 31, 32, 33, 34, 38, 43, 64, 73, 74, 76, 78, 79–80, 81, 82, 83, 84, 85, 86, 93, 95, 96, 97, 102, 103, 124, 156, 157, 160, 174, 175
Jurjina, 35, 36, 40, 172, 176
Khalili, 22, 23, 24, 33, 48, 53, 57, 172, 173, 174, 175
Khalwati, 22, 23, 30, 31, 32, 33, 34, 92, 94, 107, 129
Khanabat, 20, 30, 31, 32, 34, 37, 43, 65, 73, 76, 134, 150, 156, 161–62
Kurd, 11, 13, 14, 15, 23, 30, 32, 33, 34, 114, 178–79
Kuyani, 22, 23, 26, 31, 32, 96, 97, 180, 182, 185

Lami, 15, 22, 30, 31, 32, 34, 92, 99, 101, 102, 120
Lawouk, 22, 23, 28, 31, 32, 64, 65, 66, 67, 70, 102

Madmi, 22, 30, 31, 32, 33, 34, 35, 37, 42, 85, 104, 111, 120, 122–23, 132, 133, 163
Mahmudi, 22, 30, 31, 32, 33, 34, 43, 62, 64, 73, 74, 76, 78, 79, 81–82, 83, 84, 85, 87, 111, 129, 130, 132, 133, 157, 169, 174, 175, 180, 184
Mahur, 47, 76, 165
Mahuri, 22, 24, 32, 33, 169, 174
Mansuri, 19, 20, 22, 31, 32, 33, 34, 35, 39, 43, 47, 48, 49, 50, 56, 59, 76, 78, 92, 96, 129, 132, 134–37, 138, 139, 141, 142, 150, 151, 161, 180
Mathnawi, 21, 22, 23, 30, 31, 32, 33, 34, 47, 48, 53, 58, 59, 111, 117, 120, 122, 126, 127, 134, 136
Mischin, 22, 30, 31, 32, 33, 34, 43, 62, 63, 64, 73, 75, 76, 78, 83–84, 85, 87, 159
Mo'at, 23, 32, 33, 156, 157, 160, 174
Morabad, 21
Mthalatha, 21, 22, 23, 29, 31, 32, 33, 65, 73, 76, 79, 81, 82, 83, 85, 87, 88, 92, 102, 111, 124, 125, 132, 133, 134, 137, 139, 144, 163, 176, 180. *See also* Sereng
Muhayer, 21
Mugabl, 22, 31, 32, 33, 34, 38, 64, 73, 74, 76, 78, 79, 80, 81, 82, 83, 85–86, 111, 114, 122, 124, 132, 133, 153
Mukhalef, 21, 22, 30, 31, 32, 33, 34, 35, 38, 43, 62, 81, 87, 88, 96, 97, 102, 114, 116, 134, 139, 147, 150, 153, 155, 169, 180–86
Mukhalef Kirkuk, 21, 22, 23, 26, 30, 31, 32, 33, 96, 114, 115, 120, 138, 139, 144, 147, 149, 153, 154, 176, 177, 180, 182
Muste'ar, 22, 23, 26, 31, 114, 115, 147, 148
Muye, 180

Nagriz/Nikris, 12, 13, 14, 22, 23, 24, 31, 33, 34, 47, 51, 54, 55, 57, 104, 105, 108, 110
Nahawand, 11, 13, 14, 15, 18, 22, 23, 24, 30, 31, 32, 34, 43, 47, 48, 64, 65, 111, 120, 122, 129, 138, 147, 156, 157, 161, 162, 163–64, 165
Nahoft, 21, 22, 23, 29, 31, 32, 33, 64, 65, 71, 134, 139, 146
Nari, 18, 31, 32, 33, 34, 35, 37, 43, 47, 64, 65, 76, 77, 87–88, 176, 180
Nawruz Ajam, 21, 30, 34
Nawa, 15, 19, 20, 22, 23, 31, 32, 33, 34, 35, 39, 42, 43, 64, 65, 69, 76, 79, 81, 87, 96, 104, 105, 138, 156–60, 163, 164, 165, 172, 174
Nawa'athar, 14

Oj, 99, 117

'Omar Gala, 22, 23, 25, 30, 31, 32, 73, 76, 77, 80, 81, 82, 85, 132, 133
Orfa, 22, 23, 31, 32, 33, 34, 41, 43, 76, 79, 89, 90, 92, 96, 99, 102–3, 180

Panjgah, 12, 15, 20, 22, 32, 33, 34, 43, 47, 59–61, 62, 63, 134

Qaderbijan, 22, 26, 31, 138, 147, 149, 153, 154
Qarache, 47
Qariabash, 21, 22, 23, 25, 30, 31, 32, 65, 73, 74, 76, 78, 79, 80, 81, 82, 85, 132, 133
Qatar, 21, 22, 30, 31, 32, 33, 34, 35, 62, 63, 73, 75, 76, 78, 79, 80, 85, 86, 104, 111, 113, 124–25, 176, 177
Qatuli, 22, 27, 32, 180
Qazaz, 21, 22, 23, 25, 30, 31, 32, 34, 76, 104, 105, 109, 117, 119, 120
Quriyat, 22, 30, 31, 32, 34, 42, 43, 64, 73, 74, 76, 77, 79, 80, 81, 82, 85, 86, 87, 91, 180

Rahat Arwah, 147, 149
Rashdi, 22, 32, 33, 34, 35, 41, 43, 62, 73, 87, 129, 165, 169, 171, 172–73, 174
Rast, 11, 12, 13, 14, 15, 16, 18, 20, 21, 22, 23, 24, 31, 32, 33, 34, 35, 42, 43, 47–58, 59, 62, 64, 65, 67, 73, 75, 76, 77, 78, 83, 87, 89, 92, 134, 136, 138, 176, 177
Rast Panjgah, 76
Ruh ol-Arwah, 172
Rukbani, 22, 23, 27, 31, 33, 76, 153, 155

Saba, 14, 19, 20, 21, 22, 23, 31, 32, 33, 34, 35, 40, 43, 47, 48, 64, 65, 70, 72, 81, 92, 104, 105, 109, 110, 129–31, 132, 134, 138, 150, 153, 156, 159, 165, 168, 169, 171, 172, 173, 174, 180
Sa'idi, 21, 22, 30, 31, 32, 33, 34, 111, 112, 120, 121, 122, 123, 126, 127
Sa'idi Mubarqa, 21
Salmak, 22, 23, 27, 139, 144
Samah, 35, 36, 39, 134, 138, 156, 159, 160
Sayakhi, 64
Segah, 11, 12, 13, 15, 19, 20, 21, 22, 23, 26, 30, 31, 32, 33, 34, 35, 39, 43, 58, 76, 77, 81, 82, 85, 87, 110, 111, 113, 114, 129, 134, 138–46, 150, 153, 156, 161, 176, 177, 180
Segah Ajam, 21, 22, 27, 33, 138, 139, 142, 145
Segah Balban, 21, 22, 23, 27, 32, 33, 48, 52, 56, 139, 142
Segah Halab, 21, 22, 23, 24, 138, 139
Sengin sama'i, 36, 47, 48, 57
Sereng, 22, 29, 31, 32, 33, 157, 180. *See also* Mthalatha
Shahnaz, 21, 22, 24, 31, 104, 105, 109, 111
Sharqi Dogah, 33, 34, 35, 40, 43, 62, 64, 89–90, 92, 96 102, 172
Sharqi Rast/Sharqi Esfahan, 22, 33, 34, 40, 43, 47, 48, 51, 57, 59, 62–63, 81, 83, 89, 124, 172, 173, 174, 175, 180
Shur, 21, 43, 44n24, 47, 73, 132, 180
Shushtari, 30, 44n17
Sisani, 22, 24, 31, 176, 177
Sufyan, 22, 23, 27, 31, 32, 33, 87, 111, 139, 143, 147
Sunbule, 21, 22, 23, 28, 32, 33, 76, 77, 79, 139, 144, 156
Suznak, 15
Suz-o-godaz, 161

Taher, 20, 22, 31, 32, 33, 34, 37, 43, 62, 76, 77, 79, 81, 92, 96, 98, 129, 157, 169, 171, 172, 174–75
Tiflis, 21, 22, 30, 31, 33, 34, 45n21, 139, 145, 153, 176

'Udhdhal, 22, 23, 26, 32, 180, 182
'Ushaish, 22, 23, 25, 31, 32, 33, 89, 90, 96, 97, 98, 102, 103, 126, 127, 156, 157, 158, 160, 165, 172
'Ushshaq, 21, 22, 23, 30, 31, 117, 147, 149

Wahda, 35, 36, 40, 41, 47, 48, 62, 64, 83, 89, 96, 102, 104, 105, 108, 129, 130, 156, 157, 159

Yatimi, 22, 23, 24, 32, 162, 163
Yugrug, 35, 36, 37, 39, 64, 73, 76, 79, 81, 85, 87, 111, 122, 132, 134, 136, 138, 142, 153, 161, 169, 174, 180

Zabol, 153
Zanburi, 22, 24, 32, 76, 78
Zaza, 22, 23, 28, 32, 33, 76, 89, 102, 103

About the Author

Rob Simms worked as a freelance musician while completing his studies in music at the University of Manitoba, York University, and the University of Toronto. His research interests focus on the performer's perspective and creative processes in West Asian and West African musical traditions. He plays several instruments (including the setar, ney, and kora) and is currently Assistant Professor of Music at York University in Toronto.